ANTIQUITY REVISITED

English and French Silver-Gilt

ANTIQUITY REVISITED

English and French Silver-Gilt

FROM THE COLLECTION OF AUDREY LOVE

ANTHONY PHILLIPS
JEANNE SLOANE

CHRISTIE'S
BOOKS

First published by Christie, Manson and Woods Ltd, 1997
8 King Street
St. James's
London SW1Y 6QT
England

This book accompanies the exhibition of English and French silver-gilt from the Collection of Audrey Love at Christie's New York, September, 1997

ISBN 0-903432-50-1

British Library Cataloguing-in-Publication Data
A catalogue record for this book is available from the British Library.

Printed and bound in Great Britain by White Brothers (Printers) Ltd, Unit 1, Stockholm Road, London SE16 3LP England
Photographs by David Schlegel except where indicated
Cover design by Lynn Fylak

Front cover illustration: Detail of the Duke of York's Centerpiece, formed as Hercules Slaying the Hydra, Edward Farrell, London, 1824 (cat. no. 12)

Title page illustration: Frontispiece from Robert Adam's *Ruins of the Palace of the Emperor Diocletian, at Spalatro, in Dalmatia,* London, 1764. *Courtesy New York Public Library.*

CONTENTS

ACKNOWLEDGEMENTS

We would like to thank above all the Trustees of the Audrey B. Love Settlement for making this exhibition and catalogue possible.

A large number of people have contributed to this project. We are particularly grateful to Olivier Gaube du Gers of Maison Odiot, who could not have been more generous in providing designs, descriptions of accounts, and other information from the archives at Odiot. Equally generous has been Philippe Palasi in allowing us to be the first to reveal the results of his researches into the mysterious coats-of-arms on Odiot's celebrated Demidoff Service. We would also like to thank Ubaldo Vitali, art historian and silversmith, whose rare combination of talents is well-reflected in his essay on the history and technique of gilding on silver.

Additionally, we would like to thank Clare Le Corbeiller at the Metropolitan Museum of Art, New York, and Ellenor Alcorn of the Museum of Fine Arts, Boston. Others who have contributed research are Peter Collingridge and John Hardy of Christie's London, Andrew Butterfield and Faith Pleasanton of Christie's New York, Alain Gruber, Christie's international consultant, and Richard Bishop of Spink.

The production of this catalogue would not have been possible without photographer David Schlegel, whose knowledge of silver contributed to the design of each image. Ian Wilkie, Susan Collins, Rachel Atkinson, Genevieve Wheeler, Catrin Pride, Jessica Jewell, Laurie Schofield, and Anne Giscard d'Estaing all have helped in the most practical ways.

Our thanks are owed to our senior colleagues at Christie's New York who have encouraged this project, Christopher Burge, Patricia Hambrecht, and Stephen Lash. We also are grateful for the contributions of our colleagues in the silver departments at Christie's worldwide, in particular Thierry de Lachaise, Harry Williams-Bulkeley, Anna Eschapasse, and Christopher Hartop.

Lastly our thanks to Sara, Luke and Isobel Phillips and to Alexander Sloane for putting up with many a lost weekend.

The classical style in English and French silver-gilt

The Love Collection provides a unique opportunity to study and compare the magnificent silver-gilt objects made in England and France in the early 19th century. The emphasis of the collection on the silver of the Napoleonic and Regency periods invites an examination of the two countries' related yet distinctive styles. The best designs for both English and French silver in this period were in the classical taste, inspired by the artifacts of ancient Rome, but their stylistic contrasts appear to be the result of vastly differing patronage in the two countries, at war with each other almost continuously from 1793 to 1815. In France, the classical style was adopted by Napoleon to help forge his Imperial identity and associate him with the idealized virtues of Republican Rome. In England, to important patrons like the Prince Regent, the classical style was one of many historical revivals which seemed to represent antiquarian erudition and created an atmosphere of opulence.

Given the enduring popularity of silver of this period, which in terms of Imperial and Regal splendour has surely never been surpassed, it is remarkable how little has been written on the similarities and differences between the two.[1] Most recent scholarship has emphasized French influence on English silver, focusing on the work of Henri Auguste, Jean-Jacques Boileau, and Jean-Baptiste-Claude Odiot.

fig. 1 French silver soup tureen from the di Circello Service, maker's mark of Henri Auguste, Paris 1787, stand 21 in. (54.5 cm.) long. *Christie's photograph.*

fig. 2 Design for a soup tureen, attributed to J-J Boileau. *Courtesy the Board of Trustees of the Victoria and Albert Museum.*

fig. 3 George III silver-gilt tea urn, maker's mark of Digby Scott and Benjamin Smith, retailer's signature of Rundell, Bridge & Rundell, London 1806, 14 in. (37 cm.) high. *Christie's photograph.*

fig. 4 Design for a wine cooler, attributed to J-J Boileau. *Courtesy the Board of Trustees of the Victoria and Albert Museum.*

Auguste's work was well known and admired in England. He was one of the few silversmiths mentioned by name in the auction catalogues of the antiquarian William Beckford of 1817 and 1823, and of the Duke of York's vast silver collection in 1827. The single most influential piece of Auguste's silver in England was a pair of circular tureens of 1787, originally owned by the Marchese di Circello, Ambassador to the Court of St. James's. In 1801, Royal Goldsmiths Rundell, Bridge & Rundell, the most successful retailers of the period, acquired the tureens from di Circello, and promptly sold them to George III (fig. 1).[2] Elements of the design of Auguste's tureens reappear in both drawings and pieces of silver made under the direction of Rundell's, most notably in a tureen made for George III in 1803. [3]

Boileau was brought to England by Henry Holland to take part in the elaborate decoration of Carlton House for George IV as Prince of Wales. By the turn of the century, Boileau appears to have become a successful silver designer for Rundell's, and a number of his surviving designs show Auguste's influence (fig. 2). [4] Boileau helped popularise both classical and Egyptian designs in England; a good example is the tea urn formerly in the Love Collection, made by Scott and Smith for Rundell's (figs. 3 and 4). [5] Another example of French influence on English silver design in this period is an English tureen of 1808 by Paul Storr, also for Rundell's, based on a French example made by Odiot a few years earlier belonging to the grand service made for Napoleon's mother, *"Madame Mère,"* Letizia Bonaparte (figs. 5, 6 and 7). [6]

Despite the influence of Auguste, Boileau, and Odiot on the silver made for Rundell's, it cannot be assumed that English silver of this period is a mere

fig. 5 George III silver tureen or *coupe d'entremets*, maker's mark of Paul Storr, 1808, 11 in. (28 cm.) high. *Christie's photograph.*

fig. 6 French silver-gilt tureen or *coupe d'entremets* from the *Madame Mère* Service, maker's mark of J-B-C Odiot, Paris, 1806, 12 in. (31 cm.) high. *Christie's photograph.*

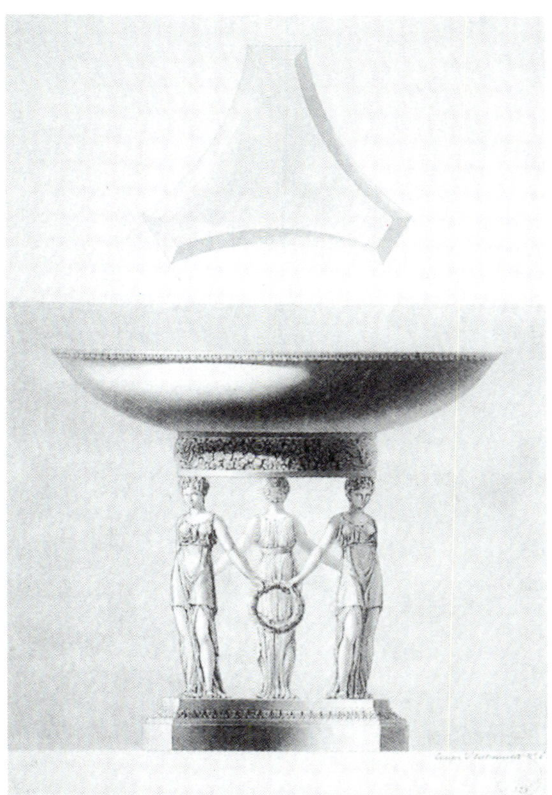

fig. 7 Design for a tureen or *coupe d'entremets* for the *Madame Mère* Service, by Auguste Moreau and A-L-M Cavelier for Odiot, circa 1806. *Courtesy Olivier Gaube du Gers, Odiot.*

derivation of the French Empire style. Indeed, the roots of the antique style had begun long before the age of Napoleon, and neoclassicism was a truly international artistic movement at least by the mid 18th century. [7] Artists and architects throughout Europe routinely studied in Rome in this period, and all had access to the numerous international publications on antiquities and classical architecture. [8] While the dissemination of styles, therefore, is extremely complex, and the design sources for French and English silver are difficult to trace, the Love Collection vividly displays the differences in the interpretations of the antique world in France and England.

Rundell's most important designer in this period was not Boileau but John Flaxman, an internationally acclaimed English sculptor who studied in Rome from 1787 to 1794, before the outbreak of war. While in Rome, Flaxman made voluminous drawings after the antique, publishing many of them as illustrations for translations of Homer, Aeschylus, and Dante. These illustrations were innovative in their severe, linear technique, which made Flaxman famous throughout Europe by the end of the century. Flaxman's "outline drawings" were highly influential to many artists and designers, including Napoleon's court painter Jacques-Louis David and his official architect Charles Percier, who also designed silver (cat. nos. 27, 28, 30 and 45). [9]

Percier and Flaxman met sometime during Flaxman's years in Rome. There, they began a professional correspondence that lasted throughout the Napoleonic Wars until at least 1820. In Paris, Percier sold Flaxman's drawings for him, and at least on one occasion in 1814, Percier distributed the drawings of Thomas Stothard, Flaxman's colleague at Rundell's. [10] During the brief period of peace following the Treaty of Amiens in 1802, Flaxman travelled to Paris to visit his friend and together they viewed the antiquities recently installed at the Louvre. [11] Percier also had assiduously studied the antiquities of Rome, and published his drawings first in *Palais et Maisons de Rome* in 1798, and also in his extremely influential *Recueil de Décorations Intérieures* of 1801-1812. Percier's designs and those of his collaborator, Pierre-François-Léonard Fontaine, were the greatest influence on the silver made by Odiot and his competitor, Martin-Guillaume Biennais. The two silversmithing firms, like Rundell's in London, retailed almost all of the important silver of their day. The Love Collection has fine examples by both makers from two of the greatest French services, the Borghese Service by Biennais and the Demidoff Service by Odiot (pp. 96-110 and pp. 129-146).

Charles Percier became Napoleon's architect in 1799, and continued to work in the strictly classical style which he had developed in Italy. The silver-gilt cruet frame in the Love Collection designed by Percier and made for Napoleon's brother-in-law, Camillo Borghese, demonstrates the essence of the French Imperial style (cat. no. 27). The figure of Nike is severely classical, and displays an almost exaggerated grandeur, given the rather pedestrian function of this object. The clarity of the design is typical of the French style, as is the consistency of the classical decoration.

By contrast, the centerpiece designed at least in part by Flaxman and acquired by the Prince Regent in 1811 exemplifies the English taste for massive pieces of silver that combine different historical styles in a single object (fig. 11). This centerpiece has a classical base supporting a surprisingly naturalistic figural group and branches. In the Love Collection, a sideboard dish marked by William Pitts, collaborator of Flaxman, centers a relief plaque based on an ancient Roman model, but the plaque is surrounded by a border in the "Dutch" floral style of the 17th century (cat. no. 8). This dish illustrates the English tendencies to draw from several periods simultaneously and also to fill undecorated surfaces, creating an eclectic and restless effect. The Prince Regent and his brothers, England's most important silver patrons, encouraged this interest in various historical styles. It is interesting to note that Flaxman had studied both medieval and Renaissance art while in Rome, filling two sketchbooks with drawings after Italian artists such as Duccio and Donatello. [12] Perhaps the Royal family's far flung tastes allowed this versatile artist to experiment outside the strictly classical vein.

Of all the Royal Dukes, it was the Duke of York who encouraged the most innovative examples of historicism. Guided by retailer and antiquarian Kensington Lewis, the Duke of York commissioned highly eclectic works from silversmith Edward Farrell. The candelabrum made for the Duke of York formed as Hercules Slaying the Hydra is Farrell's undisputed masterpiece and literally the centerpiece of the Love Collection (cat. no. 12). This monumental candelabrum draws on Italian sculpture and painting, combining designs from both the 15th and the 17th centuries, and is the ultimate example of English eclecticism. Farrell, presumably under the direction of Lewis, also looked to 17th-century German silver for inspiration (cat. nos. 17 and 18) and to the naturalistic rococo style of the 18th century. Robert Garrard II, another important silversmith and retailer of the period, also made silver in antique English styles, notably a pair of sauceboats of 1820 copied from originals in the Royal Collection of 1743 (cat. no. 11).

Even when English and French silversmiths used the same design sources, the pieces of silver produced in the two countries exhibit more differences than similarities. A case in point are three objects from the Love Collection, two English and one French, based on the engraved designs of antiquities published by Bernard de Montfaucon in Paris in 1719 and two years later in London. The two English pieces, both monumental sideboard dishes undoubtedly designed under the direction of Rundell's, have central subjects taken directly from illustrations in Montfaucon. The first dish, one of Storr's greatest works, made in 1817, has a central plaque based on a Roman cameo of Bacchus and Ariadne (cat. no. 9). The second dish, by William Pitts of 1809, has a central plaque based on a bronze relief of the Feast of the Gods, attributed to Renaissance sculptor Guglielmo della Porta (cat. no. 5). Both of these English dishes incorporate the entire engraved image in Montfaucon, with only the slightest modifications, and surround them with heavy archaeological ornament manifesting typically English *horror vacui*. By contrast, a pair of French silver-gilt wine coolers from the Demidoff Service and formerly in the Love Collection borrow from Montfaucon in an entirely different way (figs. 8, 9 and 10). For these coolers, Odiot's designer lifted a figure of a centaur out of an elaborate engraved frieze in Montfaucon and isolated it against a smooth surface, creating a more refined and severe classical object than English counterparts taken from similar engravings.

fig. 8 Design for a wine cooler, by A-L-M Cavelier for Odiot, 1816, inscribed "*approuvé*," to indicate the acceptance of the design by the client. *Courtesy Olivier Gaube du Gers, Odiot.*

The silver of this period in France and England may differ simply because the artists and patrons in both countries were reacting to the former prevailing styles. In a sense, French Empire design can be seen as a departure from the heavy, almost ponderous neoclassicism of the previous generation, most notably that of Henri Auguste's father, Robert-Joseph Auguste. In England the tendency was if anything the opposite, and designers turned away from the lightness—both in style and in weight—of the Adam style. Architect Charles Heathcote Tatham criticized this delicate manner in favour of "massiveness" in his important treatise, *Designs for Ornamental Plate* of 1806 (cat. no. 2). An economic rather than artistic factor that contributed toward the sheer weight of English silver was the explosion in wealth among the landed aristocracy, resulting from the high prices for agricultural produce during the long period of war.

fig. 9 Plate from Bernard de Montfaucon's *L'Antiquitée expliquée*, London edition, 1721. The centaur on the left is the source for the applied decoration on one side of the Demidoff wine cooler; the centaur on the right provides the decoration on the other side.

fig. 10 One of a pair of French silver-gilt wine coolers from the Demidoff Service, maker's mark of J-B-C Odiot, Paris, 1809-1819, 14 ¾ in. (37 cm.) high. *Christie's photograph.*

fig. 11 George III silver-gilt centerpiece candelabrum, maker's mark of Paul Storr, London, 1809/10, approx. 41 in. (104 cm.) high. The upper portion was designed by Flaxman and modelled by William Theed under the direction of Rundell's for the Prince of Wales. *The Royal Collection* © 1997, *Her Majesty Queen Elizabeth II.*

Napoleon's famous plunder of Roman antiquities from the conquered Papal States, installed at the Louvre in 1800, probably reinforced the French preference for a pure classical style. These well known treasures, including the Apollo Belvedere and the Laocoon, had been coveted by foreigners since the Renaissance. Louis XIV had hoped to procure for France "*tout ce qu'il y a de beau en Italie.*" [13] Napoleon's securing of these sculptures was publicly celebrated in 1798 by parading them through the streets of Paris (albeit in their packing crates), and certainly had tremendous symbolic importance for the new Empire in France. [14]

The English, who traditionally shared the fascination with ancient Rome, also had an eye on the Vatican treasures, and Nelson had been instructed to seize them when they were en route to France. [15] It is tempting to speculate that, if the Roman antiquities had arrived in England instead of France in 1798, artists there may have felt their influence to a greater degree.

In France, the classical style of the Empire remained predominant during the entire first quarter of the 19th century. The repetition of earlier designs was common (cat. no. 40), but increasingly French silver of the 1820s lacked the purity of line and the sculptural quality of that made at the height of the Empire. Following the end of Napoleon's rule, J-B-C Odiot's son, Charles-Nicolas Odiot, worked as a modeller for Garrard's from 1821 to 1823. [16] On his return to the family firm, he not only brought with him die-stamping equipment and other new technology, but also brought English designs, particularly of the rococo revival style. After he succeeded his father in 1827, C-N Odiot made silver that easily could be confused with that of English silversmiths. Indeed, the extensive dinner service he made for Count Wilhelm von Redurn in 1834 closely resembles the silver of Paul Storr's late career—a neat reversal of the situation in 1808 when Storr copied the elder Odiot's design for the *Madame Mère* tureen. [17]

1. The best treatment of the subject is Shirley Bury *et al.*, "The Nineteenth Century: Empire and Regency," in Charles Truman, ed., *Sotheby's Concise Encyclopedia of Silver,* London, 1993, pp. 107-113.
2. The pair is illustrated in E. Alfred Jones, *The Gold and Silver of Windsor Castle*, Letchworth, 1911, p. 94. Rundell's puchased a matching oval pair from di Circello at the same time, which they sold to Lord Macdonald of Slate (1773-1824). These were sold at Christie's, New York, 11 April 1995, lot 155.
3. Michael Snodin, "Jean-Jacques Boileau: A Forgotten Designer of Silver," *Connoisseur,* June 1978, p. 129.
4. *Ibid.*, pp. 125-133.
5. Christie's, New York, 14 June 1982, lot 132; also illustrated in the exhibition catalogue, *The Glory of the Goldsmith*, London, 1989, no. 121.
6. The Storr example Christie's, New York, 26 October 1982, lot 18; the Odiot example Christie's, Geneva, 16 November 1993, lot 91.
7. Robert Rosenblum, *The International Style of 1800,* New York and London, 1976.
8. Ubaldo Vitali has cited the most important of these publications; see p.15.
9. Sarah Symmons, "Flaxman and the Continent," in David Bindman, ed., *John Flaxman,* London, 1979, pp. 152-155, and Rosenblum, *op. cit.*, p. 128.
10. Sarah Symmons, *Flaxman and Europe: The Outline Illustrations and their Influence*, New York, 1984, pp. 76, 111.
11. *Ibid.*, p. 117.
12. Bindman, ed., *op. cit.*, p. 78.
13. Francis Haskell and Nicholas Penny, *Taste and the Antique: The Lure of Classical Sculpture 1500-1900,* New Haven and London, 1981, p. 37.
14. *Ibid.*, p. 111, where it is noted that this parade was intentionally held on the fourth anniversary of the fall of Robespierre.
15. *Ibid.*, p. 107.
16. We are grateful to Olivier Gaube du Gers for the specific dates of Odiot's London period; the expenses for the trip are interestingly recorded in the firm's meticulous account books.
17. Sotheby's, Geneva, 15 May 1996, lots 97-116.

A quest for the *domus aurea* in the resurgence of gilding

By Ubaldo Vitali

The Love Collection of more than 200 extraordinary objects of *vermeil*, or silver-gilt, a quarter of which are included in this exhibition, provides the scholar as well as the casual observer with a rare opportunity for the study of the art, fashion, and use of gilding. Because of the breadth of its scope, the collection sheds new light on the *milieu* which fostered the creation of such works of art. Since antiquity, gold and silver-gilt vessels had been intimately associated with royalty and godliness, but perhaps at no time in history had their symbolic value reached such magnitude as in the Napoleonic era.

During the last decades of the eighteenth century, the paths of classical archaeology and antiquarianism, fueled by a resurgence of interest in ancient writers, had wound throughout Europe with the works of such artists, scholars, and collectors as Giovanni Battista Piranesi, Robert Adam, Johann Winckelmann, Baron d'Hancarville, William Hamilton and Edward Gibbons.[1] These currents, together with an opportune political climate, set the stage from which a resurgence of the concept of the *domus aurea* or "golden house" emerged. One of the earliest accounts of this "golden syndrome" is Pliny the Elder. He recounts for us Emperor Nero's obsession with gilding as reflected on the lavish grounds of the *domus aurea*. For example, the bronze statue of Nero as the sun god which surpassed the Colossus of Rhodes by more than three metres was completely covered with gold and the seven rays that formed the statue's crown radiated its surroundings with an aura of gold, while the facade of the *domus aurea* was totally covered with gilt stuccoes. Nero had even covered the theatre of Pompei with gold just to impress Tiridate, the king of Armenia, for only a single day. Pliny then adds: *"How small was the theatre in comparison with Nero's Golden Palace which goes all round the city."* [2] Since the unearthing of the *domus aurea* in the 1480s, Nero's palace had played a crucial role in the understanding and development of the classical style based upon the vestiges of Rome. In architecture it characterized the aesthetic monumentality of this imperial style. The fresco and stucco decorations discovered in the *grotte* of the palace became a source for the decorative arts based upon a fantasmagorical mixture of plants, leaves, masks, meduse, arms, winged fish, and animals that took the name of *grottesche*.[3] First revived during the Renaissance by the school of Raphael,[4] this style of decoration quickly spread throughout Europe, maintaining its popularity well into the nineteenth century. For our purposes it is important to notice the renewed interest generated by the lengthy research of Cameron, an English architect whose publication of *The Baths of the Romans* in London 1772 included designs of the decorations in the *domus aurea*, and of the Italian publication by Carletti of *Le antiche camere delle Terme di Tito e le loro pitture* in 1776 with its illustrations of the decoration of sixteen rooms (fig. 13). Carletti's engravings had wide circulation, especially in France.[5] Images from the *domus aurea*

fig. 12 Preparatory drawing for the title page of the *XIV Cahier* of Percier and Fontaine's *Palais et Maisons de Rome*, 1798. This imaginary view was inspired by the many statues, fragments and friezes studied by the two artists during their sojurn in Rome from 1785 to 1792. The yellow wash which permeates this drawing typifies the neoclassical artist's vision of the golden aura embodied in the splendours of ancient Rome. *Courtesy Mr. Lodewijk Houthakker.*

became a lexicon for the Napoleonic style of neoclassical architects, painters, and decorators, including such cornerstones of the Napoleonic style as Charles Percier and Pierre-Francois Leonard Fontaine, whose works inspired many of the forms and decorations of the objects in this collection (fig. 12).[6]

Just as Nero in his *domus aurea* saw the incorruptibility of gold as the symbol of immortality, Napoleon also realized that his apotheosis could only take place in a *milieu d'or*. Thus, every gilt object was intended to celebrate his glory and help him to gain the majesty of an emperor. And just as Nero had built his palace upon the ruins of a burned Rome, Napoleon staged his triumphs on the spoils of that city and the plundering of her museums. The words, "Rome n'est plus dans Rome. Elle est tout a Paris," were enthusiastically sung by the masses during the processional ceremony in Paris in July 1798, celebrating the arrival of antiquities and works of art seized in Rome. However, the quest for these spoils was not restricted only to France, because Admiral Nelson had been sent in vain to intercept and seize the Napoleonic booty for England as well.[7]

This concept of the *domus aurea* continued in England, for instance, through the lavish building and gilding by the Prince Regent at Brighton Pavilion and Carlton House, as well as by his brother the Duke of York, at Lancaster House. Gold was omnipresent from the chandeliers to the plasterwork, from the draperies to the silver-gilt, and to the gilt bronze mounted furniture. Interior decoration of the Regency period, even at the "unprincely" level, reflects this quest with an increased use of yellow colour reminiscent of gold. In order to meet this demand, in 1798 Dr. Edward Bancroft introduced an inexpensive dye called *quercitron yellow*, made from the bark of the North American oak.[8]

fig. 13 Frontispiece from *Le antiche camere delle Terme di Tito e le loro pitture*, published in Rome in 1776 by the antiquarians L. Mirri and G. Carletti, showing the great attraction of the ruins to the visitors. Part of the Terme di Tito had been built upon the site of the *Domus Aurea. Avery Architectural and Fine Arts Library, Columbia University.*

Page 1

TABLEAU N° I. *Expériences citées dans le Chapitre premier.*

NUMÉROS.	SUBSTANCES MÉTALLIQUES seules ou alliées. Cuivre.	Zinc.	Étain.	Plomb.	PESANTEURS SPÉCIFIQUES.	OPINION du FONDEUR.	OPINION du CISELEUR.	OPINION du TOURNEUR.	OPINION du DOREUR.	POIDS DES PIÈCES avant la dorure.	POIDS DES PIÈCES après la dorure.	QUANTITÉ D'OR que les pièces ont reçue.
1.	100.	....	....	....	8,700.	Difficile à fondre et coulant pâteux.	Trop mou, graissant l'outil.	*Idem.*	Employant trop d'or.	137,150.	137,820.	0gr,670.
2.	70.	30.	....	....	8,443.	Coulant trop pâteux.	Bon, mais un peu mou.	*Idem.*	Bon.	142,660.	143,110.	0,450.
3.	80.	....	20.	....	8,940.	Très-facile à fondre et coulant parfaitement.	Très-mauvais et très-sec, très-cassant.	Mauvais et trop dur à couper.	Mauvaise couleur, se dérochant mal; l'amalgame s'y applique trop difficilement.	159,800.	160,260.	0,460.
4. (1)	80.	....	20.	....	8,920.	Un peu meilleur que le n° 3.	*Idem.*	*Idem.*	De même qu'au n° 3.	148,164.	148,930.	0,766.
5.	90.	....	10.	....	8,780.	Coulant un peu difficilement.	Assez bon.	Assez bon.	Mauvaise couleur, mais assez bon du reste.	141,604.	142,315.	0,711.
6.	63,70.	33,55.	2,5.	0,25.	8,395.	Bon alliage.	Bon.	Très-bon.	Très-bon, belle couleur.	148,837.	149,420.	0,583.
7.	82.	18.	3.	1,5.	8,215.	Très-bon alliage.	Très-bon.	Très-bon.	Très-bon, très-belle couleur.	143,987.	144,625.	0,638.
8.	64,45.	32,44.	0,25.	2,86.	8,542.	Très-bon alliage, comme le n° 6.	*Idem.*	*Idem.*	*Idem.*	147,010.	147,610.	0,600.
9. (2)	a.. 70,90.	24,05.	2,00.	3,05.	8,392.							
	b.. 72,43.	22,75.	1,87.	2,95.	8,275.							
10.	a.. 70,19.	26,21.	1,41.	2,19.	8,249.							
	b.. 69,87.	26,95.	1,53.	1,65.	8,262.							
11. (3)	91,40.	5,53.	1,70.	1,37.	....							
12. (4)	82,257.	17,481.	0,238.	0,024.	....							

OBSERVATIONS.

(1) L'alliage n° 4 est l'alliage n° 3 soumis à la *tr*

(2) Les alliages n° 9 *a* et *b* m'avaient été remi M. Dussaussoy comme bronzes trouvés très-bon M. Thomire.

Les alliages n° 10 *a* et *b* m'ont été remis de m mais comme échantillons de bronzes trouvés mauvai

(3) Analyse de l'alliage employé par les frères Ke

(4) Alliage proposé par M. Léonard Tournu.

La boîte n° 4 contient les huit premiers échantillons dans ce Tableau.

On voit que les pièces nos 1, 4 et 5 sont celles qui absorbé le plus d'amalgame; ce sont les patères fo en cuivre rouge, en alliage de cuivre et d'étain, soum la trempe, et en métal à canon, ce qui s'accorde bien l'opinion des ouvriers doreurs.

On ne peut pas, au reste, beaucoup compter sur les ré tats consignés dans ce Tableau, à cause des erreurs qui vent naître:

1° De la dissolution du bronze lorsqu'on passe la p au *mat;*

2°. Des inégalités dans l'application de l'amalgme;

3°. Du peu d'or que l'on met sur chaque pièce, et en augmentant à peine son poids, rend les différences peu sensibles.

On voit cependant que le doreur peut employer, grand inconvénient, le cuivre rouge et presque tous alliages de cuivre, d'étain, de zinc et de plomb, mais q n'en est pas de même du fondeur, du ciseleur, du tourn et du brunisseur, qui ont besoin de trouver certaines p priétés dans l'alliage qu'ils emploient. Il faut donc chois entre tous les alliages, celui où les qualités nécessaires trouvent réunies dans la proportion la plus convenable p satisfaire le mieux possible à toutes les conditions.

fig. 14 Chart from d'Arcet's *Memoire sur l'art de dorer le bronze au moyen de l'amalgame d'or et de mercure*, Paris, 1818, the first comprehensive and truly scientific study on bronze mercury-gilding. In this table d'Arcet analyzes the gilding of many different bronze alloys and records their evaluations by casters, spinners, chasers, and gilders.

Because of this trend in the first few decades of the nineteenth century, a large number of old silver objects were brought back to silversmiths to be gilded. Due to the scarcity of documentation, the results of this clamour of activity have created serious debate among experts regarding the authenticity of gilding. Many objects, given their use, may never have been intended to be gilt and our understanding of their original aesthetic development has been, therefore, compromised. Unfortunately, this argument cannot be addressed here, as it deserves an essay of its own.[9]

At the start of the nineteenth century the extent of the demand spurred new research towards finding a less expensive way to gild metal. Until then the most practiced method, among others, had been the so-called mercury or fire-gilding, a most dangerous technique due to the poisonous effect of mercury vapours, and a costly one because of the large amount of gold coating left by this process. The solution to this pursuit came with the discovery of an amazing new way of depositing gold by the means of an electrical current. In its simplest terms the process works as follows: the object (the cathode) to be plated is suspended in a conductive solution (the electrolyte) containing salt of the metal to be deposited and connected to the negative terminal of a Direct-Current supply. Anodes, usually of the same metal are connected to the positive terminal. Through a complex electro-chemical process, the metal from the anode dissolves into the plating solution, while some of the metal contained in the solution is transferred onto the object.[10] The early history and development of electroplating is complex and includes researchers all throughout Europe. It was also very controversial because of the exploitation of one another's investigative studies. This story culminated on March 25, 1840 with British Patent #8447 granted to George

Richards Elkington and his cousin Henry Elkington for "gold and silver electroplating."[11]

However, this method had been invented much earlier. The first recorded experiment on gold plating was published in 1802 in the *Annali di Chimica* by Luigi Brugnatelli, a professor at the University of Pavia and close friend of Alessandro Volta, professor of Natural History at the same university, and it involved an incident with Napoleon himself.[12] We could speculate that Brugnatelli's experiments may have been directly motivated by Napoleon's lust for a *milieu d'or*. In a letter to Prof. Van Mons, published in the *Annale de Chimie* in Paris in 1803, Brugnatelli describes his new discovery: *"I have recently gilt in a perfect manner two large silver medals, by bringing them into communication by means of a steel wire, with the negative pole of a voltaic pile, and keeping them, one after another, immersed in ammoniuret of gold newly made and well saturated."*[13] However, when invited along with Volta to the French Academy of Science in Paris to discuss their work, Brugnatelli was introduced to Napoleon by Volta as, *"the great Italian chemist, Brugnatelli,"* to which the emperor snidely replied, *"There are no great Italian chemists."*[14] Ultimately, the humbled scientist returned to Pavia without his method ever finding any commercial application.

It would take thirty more years of improvements, contributions and claims from scientists and *dilettanti* alike before the Elkingtons, who operated from Birmingham, a great center for metal working, transformed all these experiments into a viable commercial process and launched this new technology for industrial application. Although they immediately filed for patents in several European countries, they were met with strong opposition in France where they were granted only partial rights and they were forced to share the patent with the Comte de Ruolz-Montchal. In 1842 Charles Christofle, the founder of the famous and still extant Parisian goldsmithing firm, realized the importance of this new technology and purchased the license to the patents from both of them. With this timely acquisition he was able to establish the most important and successful nineteenth-century gold and silver plating business in France.[15]

By the 1840s, though gold electroplating had become the most viable system throughout Europe, the mercury or fire-gilding process still persisted, especially on important objects where a substantial gold thickness and a richer colour were preferred. It is important to note therefore, that the 1840s cannot be taken as the specific turning point between these two methods.

Historically, the application of a layer of gold over a lesser metal dates back at least to the third millenium B.C. Through the centuries several different techniques were devised, ranging from the early application of gold foils held in place by mechanical means, to mercury gilding, to gold cladding, through water-gilding and electroplating.[16] For centuries the most utilized method for applying a layer of gold upon a less valuable metal has been with mercury. Vitruvius, in his *De architectura* and Pliny, in his *Naturalis historia* describe the properties of mercury as well as the health hazards associated with it.[17] The two known techniques for mercury-gilding are, *cold-mercury gilding* and *fire-mercury gilding*. In the former, the surface of the object is first rubbed with mercury while cold, causing some of the base metal to dissolve, thereby forming a very thin layer of amalgam (alloy of mercury with one or more metals). Following the removal of

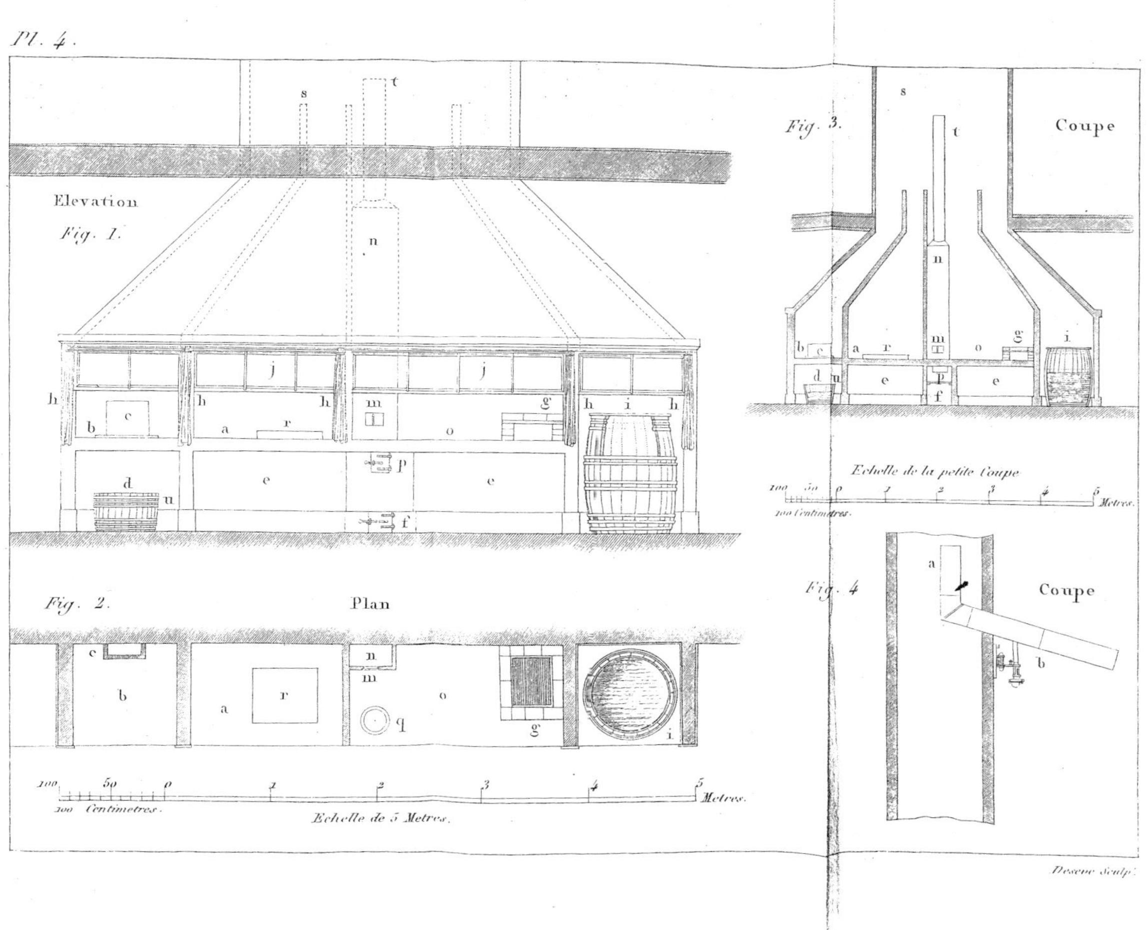

fig. 15 Plate from d'Arcet's *Memoire sur l'art de dorer le bronze au moyen de l'amalgame d'or et de mercure*, Paris, 1818, showing a system for the elimination of mercury fumes in an elevation of an actual gilder's forge in the atelier of M. d'Artois, Place des Victoires, no. 4. The forge was built and first used from October 28, 1817.

the excess mercury, a gold leaf is applied and pressed into place, absorbing some of the amalgam and firmly bonding to the base metal. Recent studies indicate that cold mercury gilding was the process most likely used in ancient Greece and Rome and as a result, a new interpretation has been placed on the writings of Vitruvius and Pliny.[18] We should emphasize that specific descriptions of this system can still be found in Renaissance treatises.[19]

The extraordinarily unusual property of mercury, also known as quick silver, had historically intrigued and fascinated the ancients. For the alchemist of the Middle Ages, however, it had become (together with sulfur), the *prima materia* and one of the essential components of the sought after *philosopher's stone*. But only through the hands of the goldsmith in fire-gilding could mercury become the effective agent by which base metal, at least in appearance, could be transmuted into gold.

Since ancient times metals had been associated with planets and the gods. Medieval and Renaissance literature is filled with passages in which mercury, the metal, is directly identified with Mercury, the god. Vannoccio Biringuccio typifies this belief in his *Pirotechnia*, the classic sixteenth-century treatise on metallurgy. *"Indeed is the sport and flirt of the alchemistic crowd, who continually stand around it* [mercury the metal] *with the desire to anatomize it, attempting sometimes with cajoleries and deceits, and sometimes with force, to put it in most narrow prisons, or to wall it in with various devices,..Yet, after all, it is one of the gods and has divine strength in itself, and also, to the annoyance of the alchemists, it is winged. Hence, when it sees that it is in grave danger, it loosens itself from their every bond in order to save its life and it flies away into the heavens...Almost laughing, it leaves all its adversaries mocked and scorned with their phials and filters empty."* Biringuccio also warns us of its dangerousness: "*...and makes the limbs of those who continually handle it weak and paralized."*[20] Benvenuto Cellini goes even further with his warning: "*I say that great masters ought not to practice this themselves, for the quick-silver that has to be used for it is a deadly poison."*[21]

Notwithstanding all of the poisonous effects of mercury, the alchemist-physician of the Renaissance used it in his many concoctions in the search for the perfect elixir to cure all ailments. Jacobo Berengario da Carpi, the famous physician and anatomist for example, used mercury for the treatment of Syphilis that was ravaging throughout sixteenth-century Europe. It should be noted that it remained the only remedy against that disease until the nineteenth century.[22]

Although earlier writings extensively refer to fire gilding, the first in-depth account of its formulae and methods appear in Theophilus Presbiter's *De diversis artibus*. In his twelfth-century treatise on painting, glassmaking, and metalworking, this Benedictine monk provides us with the details of the wide range of technical processes used in Medieval Europe. Excluding the many undecipherable alchemical writings which explored the use of mercury in transmutation, it was not until the sixteenth century that clear treatises on the subject appeared. They include Biringuccio's *Pirotechnia*, Georgius Agricola's *De re metallica*, and Benvenuto Cellini's well-known *Due trattati. uno intorno alle otto principali arti dell'oreficeria....* The following centuries witnessed a proliferation of manuals published in many languages.[23] We should note that one of the most comprehensive on this subject was the *Memoire sur l'art de dorer le bronze au moyen de l'amalgame d'or et de mercure* by M. D'Arcet, published in Paris in 1818, at the zenith of the gilding fashion (fig. 14).[24] This book was the result of intense research to eliminate the deleterious effects associated with mercury gilding, conducted by L'Academie royale des Sciences de l'Institut de France, which prompted the passage of a law requiring the adoption of the new methods described in D'Arcet's book by every Parisian bronze gilder (fig. 15).

While the description of the process seems simple enough, its execution is complex and optimum results are not easily achieved. Just as every great chef may give us his recipes but withhold the secrets of his art, so it is with the formulae as recorded in these writings. To this day the basic formula continues to be: pure gold or close to 24KT is made into extremely thin foils and cut into small pieces. Some actually prefer to grind the gold by filing it into small bits to facilitate the making of the amalgam, thus the French term, *or moulu* (ground gold). The mercury, in a proportion of approximately six parts to one gold (Cellini actually used eight to one), is placed into a crucible and heated to approximately 200°C, but not much higher because the mercury boiling point and consequently its evaporation point is 356.9°C. The gold is then also placed into this crucible and stirred until it rapidly disappears into the mercury, forming the amalgam. The solution is quickly poured into water to stop its volatization. After kneading and rinsing it, the amalgam is put into a chamois leather bag and squeezed. All of the excess mercury will filter through the pores of the leather, leaving only the gold

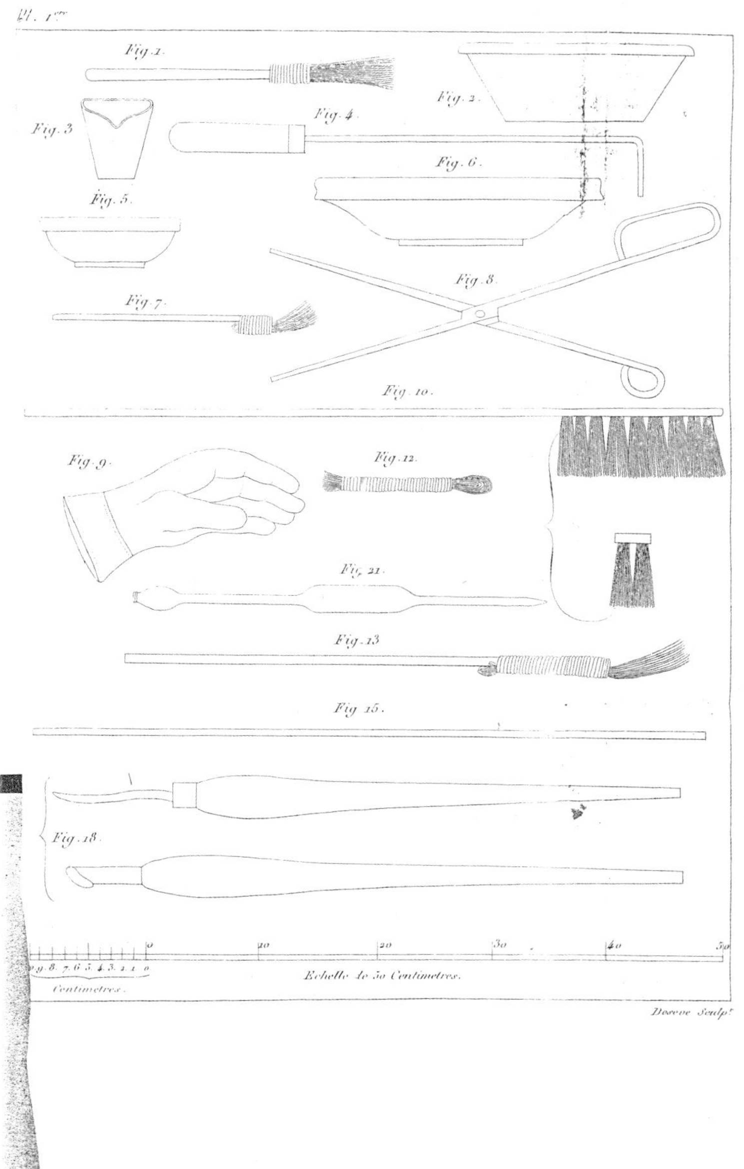

fig. 16 Plate from d'Arcet's *Memoire sur l'art de dorer le bronze au moyen de l'amalgame d'or et de mercure*, Paris, 1818, showing various tools used by the gilder.

amalgam. The amalgam retains the silvery colour of mercury and a consistency in between soft wax and thick butter. It is then divided into small equal parts, so that the gilder can know exactly the amount of gold he is using. In order to facilitate the spreading and adhesion of the amalgam, and after a thorough cleaning, the object is usually smeared with a solution of nitrate of mercury or other mercurial solutions. While heating the piece of silver over charcoal or a torch flame, the gilder applies the amalgam with various tools, such as brass wire scratch brushes, gilder's knives, spatulas, and sometimes even cork (fig. 16). The amalgam is usually laid on the *gilder stone* and is picked up with these tools which have been *quicked* into the nitrate of mercury. It is spread over the surface to be gilded making sure that it is evenly covered, and more amalgam is used if needed. Intense heat is applied until the mercury has evaporated. This is indeed a mystical and magical moment. Just as the poisonous mercurial fumes vaporize, the surface of the object is transformed from a silvery colour into a gold one. This operation can be repeated a few times to cover bare spots or to create a thicker deposit. At this stage we are left with a dull hearty yellow-greenish colour. After scratch brushing it, the hues change to a pale yellow-greenish due to the remnants of some particles of mercury. The object must now be expertly heated to the appropriate temperature until it assumes a more yellow-orange tone. Following this first phase of the process, the most secret aspect is the final colouring of the gold. It can be achieved in a multitude of ways, by covering the surface with different chemicals and at times, applying heat again. Cellini alone gives us five different recipies for colouring, one of which specifically calls for the usual Renaissance ingredient: "*You take a little urine of children or boys, put it tepid into a clean pipkin and apply it with hog sables.*" As for the length of the time to be immersed into the solution he advises: "*...and dangle it* [the object] *in for such a time as one might say an Ave Maria. After this you can pull it out and dip it back again into the hot water.*"[25] Another of his recipes calls for a longer immersion time and perhaps a stronger power of prayer: "*Then mix them* [the ingredients] *in a glazed vessel with as much water as shall make them have the consistency of a sauce, stir them over the fire with a piece of wood and let them boil for such space as you can say two Pater Noster.*"[26]

The myriad hues of gold that can be achieved in fire-gilding is almost unlimited. For instance, small quantities of other metals can be added in the making of the amalgam, such as silver or copper, to achieve a greenish or more reddish deposit. The use of different chemicals during the colouring phase can also affect the degrees of tones. The difficulty and secretiveness of this final stage is often revealed to us through documents and correspondence. For instance, from Matthew Boulton's diary we learn that as late as 1769 he was still trying to smuggle secret recipes from Paris to improve the colour of the *ormolu* objects manufactured at his Soho factory.[27]

The different finishing techniques on the metal, such as matt finish, texturing with different chasing tools, burnishing and engraving etc., can also effect the final result. In eighteenth-century France these skills reached some of their highest degrees because of their extensive use in the manufacturing of the so-called *bronzes d 'ameublement d 'or moulu*, a term encompassing not only furniture mounts but, vases, candelabra, sconces, door knobs and many other metal gilt ornaments.[28] Great masters such as Caffieri, F.T. Germain, Pitoin, Gouthière and Thomire introduced and refined many techniques. In their hands the nuances of different chasing textures and gilding finishes captured and reflected the light, and like tiny brush strokes, created a variety of pictorial effects. By the mid eighteenth century, the great *ciseleur-doreur* in France had come to achieve equal social rank and fame as famous painters, sculptors and architects.

To analyze a gilt object for the authenticity of its mercury fire-gilding is a complex task based not only on scientific data but on connoisseurship as well. Too often, in the field of the decorative arts and antiques, unfounded notions are spread and fueled by uneducated dealers and pseudo-connoisseurs, resulting in the misinterpretation of many clues. For instance, while in a qualitative spectrographic analysis the total absence of mercury indicates that it was not used in the original application of the gold (detectable traces of mercury will always remain), its presence does not guarantee an authentic fire-gilding as is often believed, because mercury can be introduced by immersion in mercuric solution both before or after electroplating.

fig. 17 Finial on a cover from a piece of the Demidoff service, J-B-C Odiot, Paris, 1818-1838.

fig. 18 Underside of the finial in fig.17, showing the gold "spills" around the edges.

Since the introduction of gold plating in 1840, the desire for a mercury-gilt look persisted and several processes were developed in an attempt to imitate it. Some solutions with mercuric salts which are electrolytical in nature offer a close and fast alternative to the conventional fire-gilding. Even the so-called gilding *spills* usually found on the edges of the ungilt part underneath the object (it was not necessary to gild areas of the object which could not be seen), should not by themselves be seen as a sign of authenticity, as is often done to this day (figs. 17 and 18). At times *spills* are imitated to give the impression of fire-gilding. Only an accurate and comprehensive study of details, data, and methodology can reveal the true genesis of the object.

Considering the historical context as discussed in this brief article, no other private collection captures the essence of the *domus aurea* as the Love Collection has. It transposes us into an era when antiquarianism was not just a fashion but the means to reconquer past majesty and splendours. Though the lexicon was formed by the works of artists such as Percier and Fontaine and others, antiquities and ancient writers provided the "codex" to follow. In his second-century work, *The Twelve Caesars*, Suetonius's description of the *domus aurea* echoed well into the early nineteenth century: *"Parts of the house were overlaid with gold and studded with precious stones and mother of pearl. All the dining-rooms had ceilings of fretted ivory, the panels of which could slide back and let rain of flowers, or perfume from hidden sprinklers, shower upon his guests... When the palace had been decorated throughout in this lavish style, Nero dedicated it, and condescended to remark: Good, now I can at last begin to live like a human being!"*[29]

1. Among their most important works are, G. B. Piranesi, *Della magnificenza ed architettura de romani*, Rome, 1761. Piranesi's work, *Vasi. candelabri. cippi sarcofagi*, Rome, 1778, contains 118 plates collected and published on the year of his death. See also, R. Adam, *Ruins of the Palace of the Emperor Diocletian. at Spalatro. in Dalmatia*, London, 1764. G. Winckelmann, *Storia delle arti del disegno presso gli antichi*, Rome, 1783-84, 3 vols., is a posthumous edition with excellent notations and indexes. See Baron d'Hancarville, *Collection of Etruscan. Greek and Roman Antiquities from the Cabinet of the Hon.ble Wm. Hamilton. His Britannick Majesty's Envov Extraordinary at the Court of Naples*, Naples, 1776, 4 vols. See also, E. Gibbon, *The History of the Decline and Fall of the Roman Empire*, London, 1776-88, 6 vols.
2. Pliny, "Natural History", (tr. H. Rackham), *Loeb Classical Library*, IX, Book XXXIII, 45, London, 1995, and for Nero's Colossus, see Book XXXIV, 45.
3. For the "golden house" of Nero, see N. Dacos, *La decouverte de la Domus Aurea et la formation des grotesques a la Renaissance*, London, 1969. See also R. Luciani, *Domus Aurea Neronis*, Rome, 1993.
4. According to Vasari, Giovanni da Udine accompanied Raphael on his visit to the *domus aurea* and the grotesques. See G. Vasari, *Le vite dei piu eccelenti pittori. scultori et architettori*, G. Milanesi, (ed), Milan, 1878-85, VI, 550-553.
5. Between 1758-69 Cameron had been charged to conduct research on the *domus aurea* by Pope Clement XIII. See CH. Cameron, *The Baths of the Romans*, London, 1772. L. Mirri and G. Carletti, *Le antiche camere delle Terme di Tito e le loro pitture*, Rome, 1776.
6. Charles Percier and Pierre-Francois-Leonard Fontaine, were sent as pensionnaire to study in Rome in 1785 and 1786. Upon their return to France they published several books on the palaces of ancient Rome. See *Palais. maisons et autres edifices modernes. dessinés à Rome*, Paris, 1798. Their work, *Recueil de décorations intérieures comprenant tout ce qui a rapport à l'ameublement...*, Paris, 1801, became the cornerstone for the offiClal Napoleonic style.
7. For an account of the removal of the antiquities from Rome and a rich bibliography, see F. Haskell and N. Penny, *Taste and the Antique*, London, 1982, pp.107-24.
8. For an illuminating discussion of the emphasis on gilding during the Regency Period, see S. Parissien, *Regency Style*, London, 1992.
9. I would like to thank Christopher Hartop for his insights in the discussions we had on this topic.
10. J. Fischer and D. E. Weimar, *Precious Metal Plating*, London, 1964.
11. For a description in great detail, see L.B. Hunt, "The History of Gold Plating," *Gold Bulletin*, VI, 1973, 16-27.
12. L. Brugnatelli, *Annali di chimica e storia naturale*, Pavia, 1802, 21: 148.
13. Van Mons, "Extrait d'une lettre de Brugnatelli," *Annales de chimie de Van Moss*, Paris, 1803.
14. C. Bocking and I.R. Christie, "Gold electroplating; A Brief Overview," *Interdisciplinary Science Reviews*, XVII, no.3, 1992, 239-43.
15.Hunt, 1973, *ibid.*
16. A. Oddy, "Gilding Through the Ages," *Gold Bulletin*, XIV, 1981, 75-9.
17. Vitruvius, "De architectura," (tr. F. Granger), *The Loeb Classical Library*, II, London, 1985, Book, VII: 117. Pliny, IX, 1995, Book XXXIII: 51, 77, 95.
18. O. Vittori, "Pliny the Elder on Gilding: A New Interpretation of his Comment," *Gold Bulletin*, XII, 1978, 35-39.
19. V. Biringuccio, *The Pirotechnia*, (tr. C. Smith and M. Gnudi), New York, 1990, 367.
20. Biringuccio, 1990, 80-1.

21. B. Cellini, *The Treatises on Goldsmithing and Sculpture*, (tr. C. Ashbee), New York, 1967, 95.
22. Berengario Jacopo da Carpi (c.1460-c.1530), famous physician and anantomist, and professor at Bologna (1502-1527), was the first to identify the heart valves and is known for his use of mercury in the treatment of syphilis.
23. Theophilus, *On divers arts*, (tr. J.G. Hawthorne and C.S. Smith), New York, 1979, 109-15iringuccio, 1990, 367, and G. Agricola, *De re metallica*, (tr. H.C. Hoover and L.H. Hoover), New York, 1950, 297-98. See also, Cellini, 1967, 96-104. Some of the earliest formulae published in English can be found in J. Stolker and G. Parker, *A Treatise of Japanning and Varnishing*, London, 1688, reprinted 1960, 64-68. See, J. Webster, *Metallographia or an History of Metals*, London, 1671, reprinted 1978, 293-329. See, P. Shaw, *A New method of Chemistry*, London, 1741, 82.
24. M. d'Arcet, *Memoire sur l'art de dorer le bronze au moyen de l'amalgame d'or et de mercure*, Paris, 1818.
25. Cellini, *op. cit.*, 98.
26. Cellini, *op. cit.*, 102.
27. N. Goodison, *Ormolu: The Work of Matthew Boulton*, London, 1974, 73, n.61.
28. See P. Verlet, "The Wallace Collection and the Study of French Eighteenth-Century Bronzes d'Ameublement," *The Burlington Magazine*, XCII, 1950, 154-57, and *Les bronzes dorés français du XVIIIe siècle*, Paris, 1987.
29. Suetonius, *The Twelve Caesars*, (tr. R. Graves), New York, 1981, 229.

History of the Love Collection

This exhibition includes the most important examples of French and English silver-gilt from the superb collection of Audrey Love and her late husband Cornelius Ruxton Love. Mr. and Mrs. Love began collecting in the 1930s, acquiring their silver mostly at auction over the course of the next forty years—a period when great silver and silver-gilt were much more frequently available on the market than today. The Love Collection is the finest of its kind in North America, exceptional for both depth and quality. Indeed, when the Metropolitan Museum of Art held the landmark exhibition, "The Arts Under Napoleon" in 1978, it was the Audrey B. Love Foundation which lent the greatest portion of the French silver-gilt.

While its strength is silver-gilt of the early 19th century, the Love Collection formerly included an exceptional group of engraved silver from the 16th century. These pieces, an Elizabethan ewer and basin of 1567 and a set of twelve matching plates, are decorated with biblical scenes that are some of the finest known examples of the art of the engraver on silver. The ewer and basin are further elaborated with remarkable portraits of the Kings and Queens of England from William the Conqueror to Elizabeth I. The engraving on the group is signed by an unidentified engraver known by his monogram "P over M" (figs. 19 and 20).[1] The original owner of the ewer, basin and plates was probably Philip Herbert (1584-1650), 4th Earl of Pembroke and 1st Earl of Montgomery. Based on a post-1639 Strasbourg control mark struck on the plates, it seems likely that they were separated from the ewer and basin in the 17th or 18th centuries, only to be reunited, albeit briefly, in the Love Collection. The ewer and basin were acquired by Mr. and Mrs. Love at the important silver auction of J. Pierpont Morgan in 1947, and are now in the permanent collection of the Museum of Fine Arts, Boston.[2] Mr. Love gave the set of plates to the Metropolitan Museum of Art, New York, in 1965.

fig. 19 Elizabeth I parcel-gilt silver ewer and basin, London, 1567, engraving signed *P* over *M*, basin 19 ¾ in. (50 cm.) diameter. *Courtesy Museum of Fine Arts, Boston.*

fig. 20 One of a set of twelve Elizabeth I parcel-gilt silver plates, probably London, circa 1567, engraving signed *P* over *M*, 7 ⅝ in. (19.5 cm.) diameter. *Courtesy The Metropolitan Museum of Art, Gift of C. Ruxton Love, 1965 (65.260.2).*

fig. 21 George III silver-gilt tea tray, maker's mark of Digby Scott and Benjamin Smith, London, 1806, 32 in. (81 cm.) long. *Courtesy The Metropolitan Museum of Art, Gift of C. Ruxton Love, 1978 (78.524.2).*

The Metropolitan Museum has been the beneficiary of numerous additional gifts from the Love Collection. The English silver includes a magnificent tea-tray by Digby Scott and Benjamin Smith of 1806 (fig. 21), a candelabrum by Paul Storr of 1813 (figs. 22 and 23), and a monumental candelabrum by Paul Storr made in 1838. [3] Mrs. Love has also given the Metropolitan Museum two extremely fine examples of French Empire silver-gilt. The first, a travelling supper-service by Martin-Guillaume Biennais, Paris, 1798-1819, is reputed to have been a gift from

fig. 22 Design for a fruit stand, attributed to Edward Hodges Baily after an unidentified artist, circa 1810. *Courtesy the Board of Trustees of the Victoria and Albert Museum.*

fig. 23 Regency silver-gilt candelabrum, maker's mark of Paul Storr, London, 1813, 32 in. (82.5 cm.)high. *Courtesy The Metropolitan Museum of Art, Gift of Audrey Love in memory of C. Ruxton Love, 1976 (76.423.2).*

fig. 24 French silver-gilt and glass travelling supper service from the Borghese Service, in thuya wood case, maker's mark of M-G Biennais, Paris, 1798-1819, 16 in. (42 cm.) high. *Courtesy The Metropolitan Museum of Art, Gift of Audrey Love in Memory of C. Ruxton Love, 1974 (74.378.1-.46).*

Napoleon to his sister Pauline Borghese upon the Emperor's return from Elba (fig. 24). Comprising over 45 individual pieces, it is a superlative example of the travelling services with which Biennais first made his name. [4] The second gift, a pair of cruets, is made by the other great French silversmith of the Empire period, Jean-Baptiste-Claude Odiot, for his important patron Nikolai Demidoff (figs. 25 and 26). The beautiful handles on these cruets are formed as Leda and the Swan, based on a drawing by Auguste Garneray after the design by Charles Percier, Napoleon's Imperial Architect. [5]

fig. 25 Design for a cruet frame for the Demidoff Service, by A.Garneray for Odiot, after a design by Charles Percier, 1817. *Courtesy Olivier Gaube du Gers, Odiot.*

fig. 26 One of a pair of French silver-gilt cruet frames from the Demidoff Service, maker's mark of J-B-C Odiot, Paris, circa 1817, 15 in. (38 cm.) high. *Courtesy The Metropolitan Museum of Art, Gift of Audrey Love in Memory of C. Ruxton Love, 1978 (78.524.2).*

fig. 27 One of a pair of French silver-gilt tureens from the Branicki Service, maker's mark of J-B-C Odiot, Paris, 1819, 16 in. (40 cm.) high. *Christie's photograph.*

fig. 28 Design for a tureen from the Branicki Service, by A-L-M Cavelier for Odiot, circa 1819. *Courtesy Olivier Gaube du Gers, Odiot.*

In 1992, in order to benefit the Bruce Museum of Greenwich, Connecticut, Mrs. Love sold at auction a pair of French silver-gilt covered tureens from Odiot's famous Branicki Service of 1819 (figs. 27 and 28). [6] Another sale at auction in 1982 included thirteen pieces of silver, six of which are now in the collection of His Excellency Mahdi Al-Tajir in London. [7] The most important pieces in this group, all from Odiot's Demidoff Service, were two pairs of wine coolers (fig. 10), a pair of wine coasters, and a pair of tureens matching the pair in this exhibition (cat. no. 43). The Love Collection also included an example of French silver-gilt from another well known service, that of Grand Duke Mikhail Pavlovitch, fourth son of Tsar Paul I. A large tray, applied with Pavlovitch's cypher and Princely Crown and attributed to Jean-Charles Cahier, Paris, 1819-1838, was sold at auction in 1995. [8]

As is evident from the current exhibition, generous gifts to museums and sales at auction have not diminished the impact of the Love Collection, which remains one of the world's greatest assemblages of silver-gilt formed in America. It is hoped that this exhibition will allow a wider public to appreciate the beauty and grandeur of gilded silver from its most spectacular period.

1. Ellenor Alcorn, " 'Some of the Kings of England Curiously Engraven': An Elizabethan Ewer and Basin in the Museum of Fine Arts, Boston," *Journal of the Museum of Fine Arts, Boston*, vol. V, 1993, pp. 66-102.
2. The Morgan Collection was sold at Parke Bernet, New York, 1 November 1947; the ewer and basin were lot 466.
3. Storr's candelabrum of 1813 matches a pair of 1815 in the Harewood Collection, sold at Christie's, London, June 30, 1965, lot 108. The candelabrum of 1838, influenced by the "Marine Service" in the Royal Collection, was from the Tollemache Collection, and then that of Vernon Hayes, sold at Sotheby's, London, 25 February 1971, lot 209.
4. Exhibited at the Metropolitan Museum of Art, New York, "The Arts under Napoleon," 6 April-30 July, 1978, cat. No. 161. Illustrated and discussed in Jacques Helft, ed., *Les Grands Orfèvres,* Paris, 1965, pp. 282-283.
5. "The Arts under Napoleon," *op. cit.,* cat. no. 159. Illustrated together with the design in J.M. Pinçon and Olivier Gaube du Gers, *Odiot l'Orfèvre,* Paris, 1990, pp. 172-173.
6. Christie's, New York, 28 April 1992, lot 31.
7. Christie's, New York, 14 June 1982, lots 131-143. The pieces now in the Al-Tajir Collection were exhibited in 1990 at Christie's, London, in the exhibition "The Glory of the Goldsmith" and are illustrated in the catalogue, nos. 21, 23, 121, and 159.
8. Anonymous sale, Christie's, Geneva, 15 May 1995, lot 136.

English
Silver-Gilt

1. A PAIR OF GEORGE III CUPS AND COVERS

Maker's mark of Richard Cooke
London, 1803

Height 17 1/2in. (44.5cm.)
Weight 414oz. (12,918gr.)

Applied with the arms, crest, and motto of Lawson

PROVENANCE
Sir Wilfrid Lawson, 10th baronet and his wife Anne, daughter of John Hartley. He died in 1806 without issue whereupon the baronetcy became extinct.

While it has not been possible to identify a specific design source for these unusual cups and covers, their sinuous bifurcated serpent handles and Greek-key band are strongly reminiscent of the work of Jean-Jacques Boileau. [1] Richard Cooke is known to have worked to Boileau's designs; his ewer of 1802 at Woburn Abbey exactly matches a drawing by Boileau. [2] In 1804, Cooke varied the design of these vases slightly for the Richmond Race Cup. [3]

Although not a great deal is known of Cooke, he registered his maker's mark at Goldsmiths' Hall in 1799. He is thought to have supplied one of the leading retailers of his day, either Rundell and Co. or Jefferies, Jones and Gilbert, and his work can occasionally be of high quality and heavy gauge. Arthur Grimwade, in his notes on Cooke, singles out for special comment "some good covered cups of semi-classical inspiration." [4] The fact that Paul Storr, Rundell's most important silversmith, made a pair of soup tureens in 1805 for Sir Wilfrid Lawson, also using applied cast arms and crest finials, suggests that Rundell's were involved in retailing the cups although the firm did not sign either the cups or the tureens (fig. 29).[5]

fig. 29 George III silver soup tureen, maker's mark of Paul Storr, London, 1805, one of a pair made for Sir Wilfrid Lawson, 16 ¼ in. long. *Courtesy Winterthur Museum, Campbell Collection of Soup Tureens at Winterthur, Gift of John T. Dorrance, Jr.*

1. Several designs are reproduced by Michael Snodin, "J-J Boileau: A Forgotten Designer of Silver," *Connoisseur,* June 1978, pp.125-133.
2. Snodin, *op. cit.,* figs. 13 and 14, p. 131.
3. Sold Christie's London, 15 July 1975, lot 65.
4. Arthur Grimwade, *London Goldsmiths 1697-1837,* London, rev.ed.1990, p.470.
5. Both formerly in the Campbell Museum, Camden, New Jersey, and now in the collection of the Winterthur Museum in Delaware. One of these tureens was in the collection of Elinor Dorrance Ingersoll and sold by Christie's, New York, 22 November 1977, lot 151.

QUOD HONESTUM UTILE

2. A GEORGE III SIDEBOARD DISH

Designed by Charles Heathcote Tatham
Modelling attributed to S. Balaam
Maker's mark of William Fountain
London, 1805
With engraved signature "TATHAM INVT. 1805"

Diameter 27 ¾in. (69.2cm.)
Weight 394oz. (12,270gr.)

With cast and applied Royal arms of George III. Also engraved with an Earl's armorials and inscription *This Ornamental Waiter was made from the allowance of Plate which was impressed to the Earl Camden as one of His Majesty's Principal Secretaries of State in 1804-1805*

PROVENANCE
John Jeffreys, 2nd Earl Camden, (1759-1840), who married Frances, daughter and heir of William Molesworth of Wenbury, Devon, in 1785. He was a Tory MP for Bath 1780-1794, Lord Lieutenant of Ireland, 1795-1798, Secretary of State for War and the Colonies, 1804-1805, and Lord President of the Council, 1805-1812. He was created 1st Marquess Camden in 1812.
The Most Hon. The Marquess Camden, Sotheby's, London, 23 January 1964, lot 95.

LITERATURE
Charles Heathcote Tatham, *Designs for Ornamental Plate,* London, 1806, pl. I.

Few works of art express the precepts of their designer better than this remarkable sideboard dish. Heavily applied with cast acanthus, the dish illustrates Tatham's fascination with ancient Roman architecture and his belief that silver should be as boldly executed. In the introduction to his book, *Designs for Ornamental Plate* of 1806, Tatham wrote "It has been much lamented by Persons high in Rank, and eminent for taste, that modern Plate has much fallen off both in design and execution from that formerly produced in this Country. Indeed, the truth of this remark is obvious for instead of Massiveness, the principal characteristic of good Plate, light and insignificant forms have prevailed to the utter exclusion of all Ornament whatever" (fig. 30).

Tatham's classicism was a reaction in part to that of Robert Adam, the most influential designer of the previous generation. Adam's delicate neo-classical style had been adapted by silversmiths for over forty years. Among these silversmiths were those working in Sheffield and Birmingham whose new manufacturing techniques reduced the amount of metal used to make silver objects. Tatham was not the first to react against the lightness of the Adam style; as early as 1785 Horace Walpole wrote, after visiting the architect Henry Holland's new Carlton House, "How sick one shall be, after this chaste palace, of Mr. Adam's gingerbread and sippets of embroidery." [1] Tatham's designs, more sculptural

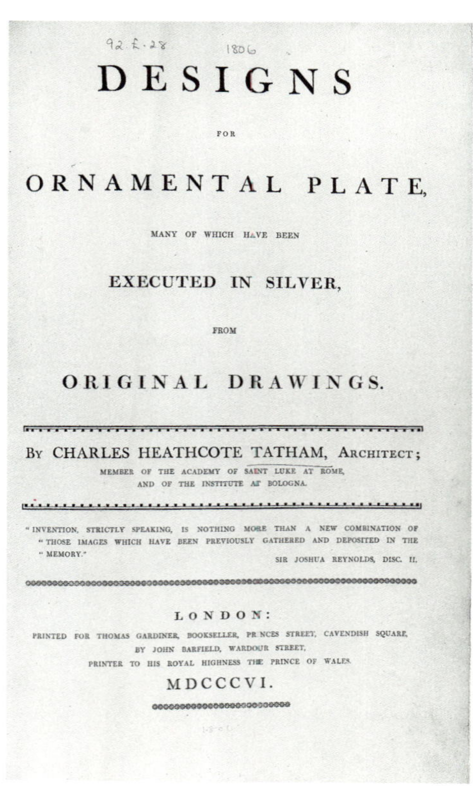
DESIGNS
FOR
ORNAMENTAL PLATE,
MANY OF WHICH HAVE BEEN
EXECUTED IN SILVER,
FROM
ORIGINAL DRAWINGS.

BY CHARLES HEATHCOTE TATHAM, ARCHITECT;
MEMBER OF THE ACADEMY OF SAINT LUKE AT ROME,
AND OF THE INSTITUTE AT BOLOGNA.

"INVENTION, STRICTLY SPEAKING, IS NOTHING MORE THAN A NEW COMBINATION OF "THOSE IMAGES WHICH HAVE BEEN PREVIOUSLY GATHERED AND DEPOSITED IN THE "MEMORY."
SIR JOSHUA REYNOLDS, DISC. II.

LONDON:
PRINTED FOR THOMAS GARDINER, BOOKSELLER, PRINCES STREET, CAVENDISH SQUARE,
BY JOHN BARFIELD, WARDOUR STREET,
PRINTER TO HIS ROYAL HIGHNESS THE PRINCE OF WALES.
MDCCCVI.

fig. 30 Title page from Charles Heathcote Tatham's *Designs for Ornamental Plate,* London, 1806. *Courtesy the Board of Trustees of the Victoria and Albert Museum.*

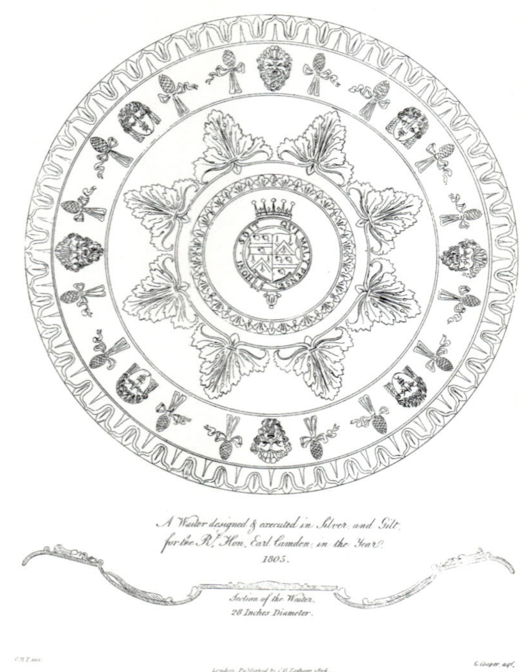

fig. 31 Plate I from Charles Heathcote Tatham's *Designs for Ornamental Plate*. London, 1806, showing design for the large dish made for Earl Camden. *Courtesy The Board of Trustees of the Victoria and Albert Museum.*

fig. 32 Plate II from Charles Heathcote Tatham's *Designs for Ornamental Plate*, London, 1806, showing design for the pair of smaller dishes made for Earl Camden. *Courtesy the Board of Trustees of the Victoria and Albert Museum.*

than Adam's and more literally taken from the antique, required a more extravagant use of metal. His archaeological approach to classicism, largely indebted to the engravings of Piranesi, was highly influential among early 19th-century silversmiths. In his other important publication *Ancient Ornamental Architecture of Rome and Italy* of 1799, Tatham wrote, "The Works of the Ancients are a MAP TO THE STUDY OF NATURE—they teach us what objects we are to select for imitation and, the method in which they may be combined for effect."

Owing perhaps to the considerable amount of metal needed in their fabrication, extant pieces of silver made to Tatham's designs are extremely scarce; only thirteen are known. The present dish is the centerpiece of a set of three dishes which includes a pair of smaller examples made en suite also for the Earl Camden in 1805.[2] The set is illustrated in Tatham's book as plates I and II, and the three are remarkably close to the designs (figs. 31 and 32). The Love dish is described as a waiter "executed in Silver, and Gilt for the Rt. Honble. Earl Camden in the Year 1806," while the pair were executed in white silver. Such mixing of silver and silver-gilt in displays of plate seems to have been an accepted practice in the early nineteenth century.

Another extant piece of silver designed by Tatham is a five-light candelabrum made for Earl Spencer at Althorp, signed TATHAM ARCHt. and marked by Thomas Pitts in 1800 which, with slight variations, appears as plate 16 in *Designs for Ornamental Plate*.[3] In addition there are nine recorded Tatham-attributed centerpieces, all by Philip Cornman dating from 1800-1813; at least three are signed by the retailers Rundell, Bridge and Rundell.[4] These centerpieces are based on elements taken from an example illustrated in *Designs for Ornamental Plate* with the caption "A piece of Plate designed and executed in Silver for the Earl of Carlisle in 1806" and also from the Althorp candelabrum mentioned above. [5]

cat. no. 2 detail

The set of three salvers, with a total weight of 876 ounces, represents an impressive allowance of "seal plate" to Earl Camden. By tradition, holders of high office were permitted to keep the silver matrices of their seals of office, either at the death of the sovereign, when the Royal arms would be defaced, or at the termination of the office. In the case of Earl Camden as Secretary of State, it seems that this perquisite was accompanied by an additional allotment of official silver. It had been customary since Elizabethan times for an official to fashion his Seal of Royal Authority into a decorative object incorporating the Royal arms, and by the 18th century, the usual result was a flat salver with an engraved likeness of the seal matrices. For the Camden seal salvers, however, Tatham's very sculptural approach to silver required fully modelled armorials which complement the other applied ornament on these massive dishes.

The modelling of the applied decoration on this dish may be confidently attributed to the sculptor Balaam, who signed one of the smaller dishes in the set of three for Earl Camden. Little is known of Balaam, but it seems likely that he is the same as the S. Balaam who in 1817 exhibited an equestrian sculpture of the Duke of Wellington at the Royal Academy. [6]

1. Horace Walpole to the Countess of Upper Ossory, 17 September 1785, as quoted in Eileen Harris, *The Furniture of Robert Adam*, London, 1963, pl. 31.
2. The pair of smaller (25in.) dishes was sold by The Most Hon. The Marquess of Camden at Sotheby's, London, 23 January 1968, lot 94 and by the Estate of Thomas Kelley, Christie's, New York, 29 April 1986, lot 150.
3. A.G. Grimwade, "Silver at Althorp," *Connoisseur*, March 1963, p. 165 fig.8.
4. Some of the centerpieces may not survive. Hilary Young cites all the recorded examples in "Philip Cornman: A Biographical Note," *The Silver Society Journal*, no.8, Autumn 1996, pp.481-486. A number of the center pieces are based on an adaptation of Tatham's design by Jean-Jacques Boileau. One of these, the Wentworth Beaumont centerpiece, is discussed and illustrated by Hilary Young, "A Further Note on J.J. Boileau, A Forgotten Designer of Silver," *Apollo*, October 1986, p.336 and fig. 6 (sold, with six matching dessert-stands, at Christie's, London, 24 June 1981, lots 22-24, and 9 July 1991, lot 77).
5. David Udy, "The Influence of Charles Heathcote Tatham," *Proceedings of the Silver Society*, vol. II, no. 5/6, Autumn, 1975, pp. 104-105.
6. E. Benezit, *Dictionnaire des Peintres, Sculpteurs, Dessinateurs et Graveurs*, Paris, rev.ed. 1976, p.392. Hilary Young, in "Philip Cornman: a Biographical Note," The Silver Society Journal, no.8, Autumn 1996, pp.481-486, suggests that Balaam's name appears at the bottom of Tatham's bill for the Earl of Carlisle's centerpiece, but it is now thought that the word is in fact "Balance,"and the total of the charges confirms this reading.

3. A PAIR OF GEORGE III SALT CELLARS

Maker's mark of Joseph Preedy
London, 1802

Length 6in. (15.3 cm.)
Weight 41oz. (1,301 gr.)

Engraved with the Royal badge

Formed as conch shells on dolphin bases chased with crabs and shellfish, these salt cellars are exceptionally early examples of marine motifs in 19th-century silver. It is perhaps significant that their maker, Joseph Preedy, was the partner from 1791 to 1799 of William Pitts, one of the most original and creative silversmiths of the first two decades of the 19th century (cat. no. 5).

4. A GEORGE III CENTERPIECE BASE

Maker's mark of Paul Storr
London, 1809
Stamped with retailer's signature *RUNDELL, BRIDGE ET RUNDELL AURIFICES REGIS ET PRINCIPIS WALLIAE LONDINI FECERUNT*

Height 21 ½in. (54.6cm.)
Weight 571oz. (17,785gr.)

PROVENANCE
Sold anonymously, Christie's, London, 19 May 1965, lot 99

The proportions of this centerpiece and remarkably plain ring for the central dish indicate that it has been in some way reduced in size. It is particularly interesting to note that this centerpiece is almost identical to the bases for a monumental pair of candelabra also by Storr for Rundell's, acquired by the Prince of Wales, and dated 1809/10 (fig. 11). [1] John Flaxman designed at least the upper portion of the Royal candelabra, and a number of drawings for them are now in the Victoria & Albert Museum. [2] One candelabrum is formed as Mercury presenting the infant Bacchus to the Nymphs at Nysa. Flaxman designed the other candelabrum as the Serpent Ladens guarding the tree of the Golden Apples of the Hesperides, being fed by the daughters of Erebus and Night. Both candelabra were modelled by William Theed, whose friend Joseph Faringdon remarked after visiting the sculptor's studio that he had seen "several of His models: Candelabrums for the Prince of Wales & other works." [3] The original design by Flaxman incorporates a base with three seated panthers around a shorter foliate stem, which was followed almost exactly by Storr, again for Rundell's, for a "Mercury" candelabrum of 1816 formerly in the collection of Sir R. V. Sutton, Bt. and for a "Hesperides" candelabrum at Goldsmiths' Hall. [4] For their Royal patron, however, Rundell's decided on much larger and grander bases with massive central stems flanked by three seated figures of Pan, which match those on the present example.

The candelabra supplied to the Prince of Wales are described in the original account from Rundell, Bridge and Rundell as:

> 2 rich candelabras to fit occasionally on tripod stands, composed from designs made by Flaxman on the subject of Mercury presenting Bacchus to the nymphs. The other the serpents guarding the tree of Hesperides, with elegant falling branches and ornamented devices. 917oz. 10dwt., Fashion 17s oz., gilding £132 each,=£1,365. [5]

The use in the account of the word "occasionally" implies that the bases were intended to be used both as supports for the larger candelabra and also alone as centerpieces fitted with glass bowls. [6]

1. E. Alfred Jones, *The Gold and Silver of Windsor Castle*, Letchworth, 1911, pls. LIX and LX.
2. Victoria and Albert Museum, London, CA1 989 and 970; E 3037/8-1927. Two are illustrated in Shirley Bury, "Flaxman as a Designer of Silverwork," in David Bindman, ed., *John Flaxman*, London, 1979, figs. 65a, 65b., 192, pp. 141 and 149.
3. As quoted by Bury, *op. cit.*, p. 141
4. Sold Christie's, London, 31 March 1976, lot 130. The "Hesperides" candelabrum on the base designed by Flaxman with the maker's mark of Philip Rundell, 1821, with branches by John Bridge, 1830, is in the collection of the Worshipful Company of Goldsmiths, London (Bury, *op.cit.*, fig. 185a, p. 144).
5. As quoted by E. Alfred Jones, *op. cit.*, p.116. According to Bury, *op. cit.*, no. 185, the two candelabra including bases were acquired by the Prince of Wales in June 1811 at a total cost of £4000/15s
6. The branches on the present centerpiece are unmarked and apparently later.

RUNDELL BRIDGE ET RUNDELL AURIFICES REGIS ET PRINCIPIS WALLIÆ LONDINI FECERUNT

5. A GEORGE III SIDEBOARD DISH

Maker's mark of William Pitts
London, 1809

Diameter 25in. (63.5cm.)
Weight 247oz. (7,684gr.)

This magnificent dish, with its cast central scene of the Feast of the Gods, is one of a series made by William Pitts, all probably retailed by Rundell's. [1] It is an extremely early example, pre-dating Farrell's work by half a dozen years or so, of a silversmith working in the Renaissance style.

Pitts made a pair of virtually identical dishes of 1810 and 1812 for the Prince Regent, supplied by Rundell, Bridge and Rundell. They differ from the present example only in the inclusion of an inner border of Vitruvian scrolls. In Rundell's account of 1812 one of the dishes is described as

> A richly chased sideboard dish, to match His Royal Highnesses, and with devices of the Feast of the Gods, from a design of Michael Angelo, with chased mosaic border, 284 oz. 15 dwt., fashion 12s.oz.= £291/17/4.; engraving crest and coronet, 9s; gilding all over dead and red, £96. [2]

In spite of the statement in the Rundell's account that the "Feast of the Gods [was] from a design of Michael Angelo," the actual design source for the central relief is a bronze plaque existing in three known versions, attributed alternatively to Alessandro Vittoria or Guglielmo della Porta, a Roman follower of Michelangelo (fig. 33). [3] However, Rundell's direct source was almost certainly an engraving of this plaque in Bernard de Montfaucon's *L'Antiquité expliquée et representée en figures*, a highly influential series of volumes first published in Paris in 1719, and translated for an English edition in 1721 (fig. 34.). [4] Montfaucon was a Benedictine scholar from the congregation of Saint Maur, whose travels in Italy from 1698 to 1701 led to his ambitious compilation of all images of antiquities known in his time. The fact that the present relief was a Renaissance and not an ancient Roman work was unknown to Montfaucon, who erroneously included later works based on antique themes as well as outright forgeries in *L'Antiquité expliquée.* [5] We can be almost certain that Rundell's owned a copy of Montfaucon, as another engraving from his book provides the subject for the relief plaque applied to another dish in the Love Collection designed by Stothard for Rundell's (cat. no. 9).

William Pitts Senior was the son of the well-known epergne maker Thomas Pitts. From 1791 to 1799, William was in partnership with Joseph Preedy, producing fine neoclassical dessert-stands and other wares but in 1799 and 1806 he registered alone at Goldsmiths' Hall, entering his own mark. In 1806 his son, also William, joined him as an apprentice and by 1812 had become an important modeller and chaser in his own right. The son is known to have worked both on Stothard's famous Wellington Shield made for the retailer Green, Ward and Green and on Flaxman's Shield of Achilles for Rundell's. [6]

William Pitts Senior seems to have decided to cater to the increasing interest in what could be called "antique" silver sometime around 1808. The fashion for old silver existed at least as early as the 1780s and no doubt before. In 1786, a Swiss visitor to London, Sophie von la Roche, wrote of her visit to royal goldsmiths Jefferys and Jones "[the] stock must be worth millions. I have never seen silver moulded into such noble, charming, simple forms...with the added pleasure of comparing the works of previous generations with-up-to date modern creations. These antique pieces, so Mr Jeffries said, often find a purchaser more readily than modern. This is because the English are fond of constructing whole portions of their country houses...in old Gothic style and so are glad to purchase any accessions dating from the same or similar period." [7]

It was the saleability of old silver that no doubt in 1808 led Rundell's not to melt, but rather to refurbish (in some cases) and sell a quantity of silver belonging to the Royal family. In order to pay for a new service of plate for Princess Caroline, the separated wife of the Prince Regent, the Jewel House selected and sold to Rundell's old silver that was considered "neither suitable for service nor valuable for its antiquity or workmanship." [8] The appearance of this group of silver with its exalted provenance on the retail market may well have stimulated further interest in antique silver. Certainly the pieces seem

fig. 33 The Feast of the Gods, a bronze plaque attributed to Guglielmo della Porta, circa 1575, 13 ⅜ in. high. *Courtesy the Board of Trustees of the Victoria and Albert Museum.*

fig. 34 Plate from Bernard de Montfaucon's *L'Antiquitée Expliquée,* London edition, 1721, based on one of the three known Renaissance bronze versions of the Feast of the Gods, thought by Montfaucon to date from antiquity.

to have been been eagerly snapped-up by important Rundell's clients such as the Earl of Lonsdale.

Given this growing demand for old plate, it is not surprising that retailers very quickly saw the potential market not only for antique silver but also for new silver made in the antique style, and it seems that William Pitts was one of the first suppliers of such pieces. It is ironic that the market for historic plate was stimulated by the sale of silver on behalf of the Prince Regent, who soon became one of the greatest patrons of new silver in antique styles, together with his brothers, the Dukes of York, Sussex, and Cambridge.

1. In addition to the two Royal dishes described below and the Love example, there are four other dishes by Pitts with the Feast of the Gods relief: one of 1809 formerly in the collection of the Dukes of Ormonde, presently at Brighton Pavilion (acc. no. 344197); another of the same year in the Al-Tajir Collection, illustrated in *The Glory of the Goldsmith,* London, 1989, no.127, pp.164-165; a third of 1820 with a border of applied putti, sold at Sotheby's, New York, 12 December 1973, lot 240 and illustrated in Vanessa Brett, *The Sotheby's Directory of Silver,* London, 1986, fig.1177, p.259; the fourth, almost identical to the present example and made in the same year was sold at Sotheby's, London, 22 November 1984, lot 103.
2. As quoted in E. Alfred Jones, *The Gold and Silver of Windsor Castle,* Letchworth, 1911, p.114. The dish is illustrated in pl. LVIII.
3. Anthony Radcliffe has recently attributed the plaque to della Porta. See *Carlton House: The Past Glories of George IV's Palace,* London 1991, cat. no. 73, p.119.
4. Anthony Radcliffe has observed that Pitts's Feast of the Gods related more closely to Montfaucon's engraving than to known versions in bronze. *Ibid,* p.119.
5. Francis Haskell and Nicholas Penny, *Taste and the Antique: The Lure of Classical Sculpture 1500-1900,* New Haven and London, 1981, p.43.
6. For a full discussion of William Pitts, father and son, see Sotheby's, London, 23 May 1991, lot 243.
7. Quoted by Arthur Grimwade, "Two Great Royal Sales," *Christie's Review of the Season,* 1975, p. 194.
8. *Ibid,* p. 194.

6. A SET OF FOUR REGENCY SALT CELLARS

Design attributed to William Theed
Maker's mark of William Pitts
London, 1813

Length 4 ½ in. (11.4 cm.)
Weight 78oz. (2,450 gr.)

The similarity of these salt cellars to a bronze sculpture by William Theed suggests that Theed, a sculptor who worked for Rundell's from 1803 to 1817, designed the present salt cellars and the two similar known variations of this model. The other versions of this design include one with a rectangular base matching a drawing by E. H. Baily after Theed (cat. no. 7), and another, probably later, model with a heavier base. [1] Most of the known examples are marked by Paul Storr, but William Pitts also worked for Rundell's, and it is reasonable to assume that Rundell's, who owned the drawing for the related model, commissioned Pitts to make the present salt cellars.

Rundell's supplied a set of twenty-four salt cellars of the present model to the Prince Regent in 1811, charging £902 12s. [2]

1. A set of eight of 1822 with the heavier base, marked by Paul Storr, are in the Al-Tajir Collection, illustrated in the exhibition catalogue, *The Glory of the Goldsmith*, London, 1989, cat. no. 151, p. 198.
2. The salt cellars, marked by Storr in 1810, remain in the Royal Collection (one is illustrated in *Carlton House: The Past Glories of George IV's Palace*, London, 1991, fig. 95, p. 133). A further set of four of this model was sold at Sotheby's, London, 28 February 1991, lot 83.

7. A SET OF EIGHT GEORGE III SALT CELLARS

Design attributed to William Theed
Maker's mark of Paul Storr
London, 1810

Height 4 ¼in. (10.8cm.)
Weight 166 oz. (5,186gr.)

PROVENANCE
The Duke of Westminster, Sotheby's, London, 2 July 1959, lot 129
The Plohn Collection, Part 2, Sotheby's, London, 15 October 1970, lots 82 and 83

The design for these salt cellars is attributable to William Theed on the basis of their close similarity to Theed's bronze sculpture, "Thetis returning from Vulcan with Arms for Achilles" now in the Royal Collection. [1] A number of different bases were used by Storr for this model. [2]

The attribution is further strengthened by the inclusion of a drawing for this model in an album of designs for Rundell's entitled "Designs for plate by John Flaxman, etc." (fig. 35). This book was purchased by the Victoria and Albert Museum in 1964 and studied in considerable depth by the late Charles Oman. [3] The painter and sculptor William Theed (1764-1817) was engaged by Rundell, Bridge and Rundell in 1803 to supply designs and work as their chief modeller. He had previously worked for Josiah Wedgwood as had his friend and later fellow designer for Rundell's, John Flaxman. Theed is almost certainly responsible for the modelling of several of John Flaxman's designs, including the candelabrum of 1809, formed as Mercury presenting the infant Bacchus to the Nymphs, now in the Royal Collection. [4]

Theed was initially an associate, and later a partner, in the firm of Rundell, Bridge and Rundell, remaining as such until his death in 1817. Oman came to the conclusion that all the designs in the book mentioned above were in fact drawn by John Flaxman's pupil Edward Hodges Baily, who joined Rundell's in 1815. [5] While in some cases they appear to be entirely new designs by Baily, in others they appear to have been carried out in collaboration with, or as re-workings of, other designers' work. In any event, given the date of these salt-cellars five years prior to Baily joining Rundell's, and their close relationship to the decoration on Theed's bronze "Thetis" sculpture, there can be little doubt as to the creator of the original design.

Also of interest in the Love Collection are a set of four similarly formed salt-cellars with the maker's mark of William Pitts, London, 1813, which have oval bases (cat. no. 6). While Rundell's employed Storr on a full-time basis, they are known to have also paid the two William Pitts, both father and son, for work on special commissions.

1. The sculpture, dated 1812, was included The Royal Academy of Arts Bicentenary Exhibition in 1969 and was illustrated in the catalogue, fig. 171, p.50.
2. Three are illustrated by Joseph Bliss, *The Jerome and Rita Gans Collection of English Silver on Loan to the Virginia Museum of Fine Arts*, n.d., cat. no. 37, which have oval bases chased with wave ornament. These models of 1811 are somewhat similar to the examples by William Pitts included in the current catalogue (cat.no. 6).
3. Charles Oman, "A Problem of Artistic Responsibility: The Firm of Rundell, Bridge & Rundell," *Apollo*, January 1966, pp. 174-183.
4. Shirley Bury, "Flaxman as a Designer of Silverwork," in David Bindman, ed., *John Flaxman*, London, 1979, pp. 141 and 149.
5. Oman, *op. cit.*, p. 181.

fig. 35 Design for a salt cellar, attributed to William Theed, from Rundell's book of drawings titled "Designs for Plate by John Flaxman, etc." *Courtesy the Board of Trustees of the Victoria and Albert Museum.*

8. A REGENCY SIDEBOARD DISH

Maker's mark of William Pitts
London, 1814

Diameter 22in. (56cm.)
Weight 206 oz. (6,407 gr.)

PROVENANCE
Mrs. C. Kisielewska Dunbar, Sotheby's, London, 11 June 1970, lot 237

LITERATURE
Vanessa Brett, *The Sotheby's Directory of Silver,* London, 1976, p.259, no.1176

Although this dish typifies Pitts's interest in combining design elements from various antique sources, it has a rather discordant effect when compared to Pitts's other dish in historicist style in the Love Collection (cat. no. 5). The unmarked rectangular plaque in the center of the present dish appears to be a casting from a late 17th-century relief of the Rape of the Sabines, based in turn on an antique model, possibly a battle scene from a Roman sarcophagus. Two other dishes by the same maker of 1810, now in the Royal Collection, include earlier plaques, one hallmarked in 1678, the other with the maker's mark of Jacob Bodendick, an important silversmith who came to England at the time of the Restoration. [1] Pitts seems to have been one of the first 19th-century silversmiths to incorporate antique plaques (or castings from them) in his work. Edward Farrell was also to do this on a number of occasions as was William Elliot in the 1820s. [2]

The band of repoussé foliage and flowerheads in 17th-century style around the well of this dish is a repetition of a decorative element apparently first used by Pitts on a dish of 1809 and then on the two Royal dishes mentioned above. [3] The border of the present dish, within a gadrooned rim in the German style of circa 1700, comprises cast panels with classical scenes: the Banquet of the Gods with Ganymede presenting Jupiter with a cup, Hercules embracing Omphale, and the Gods on Mount Olympus with Apollo playing the lyre.

1. E. Alfred Jones, *The Gold and Silver of Windsor Castle,* Letchworth, 1911, p.194, pl. XCVIII. It is interesting to note that plaques with identical scenes to those incorporated in the Pitts's Royal dishes (Phaeton pleading with his father and Phaeton plunging to Earth with his sisters turning their grief into poplar trees) are found in the covers of two cylindrical toilet boxes in the Morgan dressing-table service of 1683 (sold at Christie's, New York, 26 October 1982, lot 53, now in the Al-Tajir collection). The Morgan service is now known to be by William Ffowle (for the identification of this maker and his working relationship with Jacob Bodendick see David Mitchell, "Dressing plate by the 'unknown' maker WF," *The Burlington Magazine,* June 1993, pp.386-400.) Ffowle also used the plaque of Phaeton pleading with his father in the cresting of the mirror in the well-known Calverly Service in the Victoria and Albert Museum.
2. Examples by Farrell include a sideboard dish of 1822 with a signed 17th century plaque (sold at Sotheby's, London 20 June 1974, lot 57, and illustrated by Vanessa Brett, *The Sotheby's Directory of Silver*, London, 1986, no.1241) and a pair of pilgrim bottles of 1825 with 17th century English and Dutch plaques (illustrated in Timothy Schroder, *The Gilbert Collection of Gold and Silver*, Los Angeles, 1988, pp.452-458, no.122). Examples by William Elliot are fairly numerous (e.g., Brett, *op.cit,* no.1252), and his caskets are often engraved with inscriptions stating that they "have been made to receive a chas'd medallion of unknown assay."
3. For an example of 1809, sold at Sotheby's, London, 7 June 1979, lot 71, see Brett, *op.cit.,* no.1175.

9. A REGENCY SIDEBOARD DISH

Designed by Thomas Stothard
Maker's mark of Paul Storr
London, 1817

Diameter 31in. (78.7cm.)
Weight 357oz. (11,107 gr.)

Engraved with the arms of Brudenell-Bruce impaling Noel-Hill

PROVENANCE
Charles Brudenell-Bruce, 2nd Earl of Ailesbury (1733-1856) and his wife Henrietta Maria, daughter of Noel (Hill), 1st Lord Berwick of Attingham. In 1821, the second Earl was created 1st Marquess of Ailesbury, one of the coronation peerages of George IV
The Marquess of Ailesbury, Christie's, London, 15 November 1944, lot 76
Sir William Butlin, Christie's, London, 17 July 1968, lot 42

LITERATURE
Christie's Review of the Year, 1967-1968, London, 1968, pp.144-145
Michael Clayton, *Christie's Pictorial History of English and American Silver,* London, 1985, fig.4, p.259

One of the great masterpieces of the Love Collection and indeed of Regency silver-gilt as a whole, this dish was one of a series based on a drawing by Thomas Stothard for Paul Storr's workshop under the direction of retailers Rundell, Bridge and Rundell. In her biography of Thomas Stothard published in 1851, Stothard's daughter-in-law Anna Eliza Stothard Bray describes the design of the present dish, recounting that Stothard "chose for his subject Bacchus and Ariadne, drawn in a chariot by Satyrs. This was imagined and delineated with true classic taste and feeling. All these drawings were most elaborately finished in sepia" (fig. 38). [1] The survival of Stothard's pen-and-wash rendering at the Victoria and Albert Museum, combined with Bray's suggestion that the subject was of the artist's own imagination, has led scholars to conclude that the Bacchus and Ariadne scene was Stothard's original design, although strongly influenced by John Flaxman. [2] However, the actual source of Stothard's central relief, previously unrecognized, was an engraving in Bernard de Montfaucon's *L'Antiquitée expliquée* of 1719, an encyclopedic compilation of ancient works of art, a copy of which was undoubtedly owned by Rundell's (fig. 37). [3] The subject of Montfaucon's engraving was a celebrated antique Roman cameo excavated in the Via Aurelia in 1661 (fig. 36). This cameo was acquired successively by Cardinals Massimo (d.1677) and Carpegna (d.1714), and its archaeological significance is underscored by the fact that it was engraved and published twice in the 17th century. Montfaucon's engraving was in fact based on a previous print by F. Buonarotti in *Osservazioni Istoriche,* Rome, 1698. Pope Benoit XIV purchased the cameo in 1741, and it remained in the Vatican until it was seized by Napoleon in 1798. It arrived in Paris in 1801, and remains today at the Louvre. [4]

Stothard's copy of the Triumph of Bacchus cameo is quite literal, although he adjusted the rectangular composition to fit a circular format, added a lyre and two putti, and changed some minor details. While not, therefore, an interpretation of a Flaxman design, Stothard's selection of this relief as his source nonetheless is probably indebted to Flaxman's familiarity with Roman antiquities newly arrived in Paris at the time. Throughout the Napoleonic wars, Flaxman maintained a correspondence with Imperial architect Charles Percier, whom he had met at Rome. In 1802, the peace following the Treaty of Amiens allowed Flaxman to visit Percier in Paris, where together they examined the superb antiquities recently installed at the Louvre by Napoleon. [5] It is entirely likely that Flaxman saw the famous Bacchus and Ariadne cameo then. Whether or not Stothard himself travelled to Paris is not known, but it is

fig. 36 Antique Roman marble cameo, mounted in ormolu and hardstone frame by Luigi Valadier for Pius VI in 1780, cameo 16 in. (41 cm.) long. The cameo was among the Vatican's antiquities seized by Napoleon and installed at the Louvre in 1800. *Collection Musée du Louvre; photograph by Chuzeville, Réunion des Musées Nationaux, France.*

documented that Percier knew of him. In 1814, Percier received some engravings by Stothard from Flaxman, and sent his thanks for the work "*de votre célèbre ami M.Stothard.*" [6]

Stothard used the Triumph of Bacchus cameo in at least one other design for silver. A pen-and-wash rendering of a wine cooler, now at the British Museum, employs the same four centaurs, intended for execution as fully-modelled figures arranged around a central vase. [7] This rather inharmonious design was apparently never executed.

Other sideboard dishes from Stothard's Bacchus and Ariadne series include an example of 1814 by Paul Storr sold to the Prince Regent by Rundell, Bridge and Rundell and described in their invoice of 1815 as

> A large round and very superb sideboard dish with the story of Bacchus and Ariadne, drawn by centaurs finely chased in high relief, with a rich chased vine and grape border with bacchanalian masks, all of the best workmanship. 365oz. 1dwt., fashion 18s. 6d. oz=£497 7s 7d.; engraving the royal arms, 18s.; gilding all over in the best manner, £118." [8]

fig. 37 Plate from Bernard de Montfaucon's *L'Antiquitée Expliquée*, London edition, 1721, based on the antique cameo excavated in Rome in 1661 and engraved by F. Buonarotti in 1698, illustrated as fig. 36.

The earliest known sideboard dishes made to this design are a pair of 1813 made by Storr for Rundell's for Hugh, 3rd Duke of Northumberland. [9] Although slightly larger than the Royal and Love sideboard dishes, this pair is arguably of somewhat weaker design, with low-relief musical instruments on the borders instead of bold bacchanalian masks. The pair is known to have been re-acquired by Rundell's from the Earl of Tylney's sale at Wanstead House, Essex, June 18, 1822 at a cost of £252 7s for one and £255 3s for the other.

The success of Stothard's Bacchus and Ariadne dish may have led to his obtaining the commission for the famous Wellington Shield. According to *The Art Journal*, the shield was designed shortly before Waterloo, apparently in 1814, and "the work was competed for by the London goldsmiths all of whom are said to have applied to Stothard for a design." [10] Stothard supplied the retailers Green, Ward, and Green with the design and it was made for them by Benjamin Smith. Completed in 1822, it was presented by the Merchants and Bankers of the City of London to the Duke of Wellington and is still displayed at Apsley House.

1. A.E.Bray, *Life of Thomas Stothard, R.A.*, London: John Murray, 1851, p.162.
2. See David Irwin, "Royal Plate and Other Metalwork," in *John Flaxman 1755-1826*, New York, 1979, pp.194-196.
3. Another dish made for Rundell's with a plaque based on Montfaucon is in the Love collection (cat. no. 5).
4. The cameo was mounted in an ormolu and hardstone stand by Valadier for Pius VI in 1780. See Alvar González-Palacios, "Triomphe de Bacchus," *Luigi Valadier au Louvre, ou l'Antiquité Exaltée*, Paris, 1994, pp. 51-59.

fig. 38 Thomas Stothard's pen-and-wash rendering of the Triumph of Bacchus Cameo, after Montfaucon's engraving. *Courtesy the Board of Trustees of the Victoria and Albert Museum.*

5. Sarah Symmons, *Flaxman and Europe: the Outline Illustrations and their Influence,* New York, 1984, pp. 73-117.
6. *Ibid.,* p. 76.
7. Charles Oman, "A Problem of Artistic Responsibility," *Apollo,* January 1966, p. 176, fig.5.
8. Quoted By E. Alfred Jones, *The Gold and Silver of Windsor Castle,* Letchworth, 1911, p. 124. The dish is illustrated as pl. LXIII.
9. Sold by His Grace the Duke of Northumberland, Sotheby's, London, 3 May 1984, lot 105. Illustrated by Vanessa Brett, *The Sotheby's Directory of Silver,* London, 1986, p.254 fig.1146. They are now in the Al-Tajir Collection, included in the exhibition catalogue, *The Glory of the Goldsmith,* London, 1989, p.183.
10. *The Art Journal,* 1894, p. 87, as quoted by John Culme, *Nineteenth-Century Silver,* London, 1977, p. 61. The shield itself is illustrated in Shirley Bury, "The Lengthening Shadow of Rundell's Part 1: Rundell's and their Silversmiths," *Connoisseur,* February, 1966, fig. 3.

10. A GEORGE IV SIDEBOARD DISH

Design attributed to Benedetto Pistrucci
Maker's mark of Philip Rundell
London, 1820
Stamped with retailer's signature *RUNDELL, BRIDGE ET RUNDELL AURIFICES REGIS LONDINI*

Diameter 31in. (78.8cm.)
Weight 482 oz. (15,029 gr.)

Applied with the arms of Goldsmid impaling Goldsmid

PROVENANCE
Sir Isaac-Lyon Goldsmid, 1st Baronet (1778-1859) who married in 1804 his cousin Isabel, daughter of Abraham Goldsmid. Sir Isaac-Lyon devoted his life to the cause of Jewish emancipation and he became the first baronet of that faith in 1841.
Mrs. Garside, Christie's, London, 31 January 1968, lot 53

LITERATURE
Christie's Review of the Year, 1967-1968, pp.144-145

This superb dish is related to Stothard's Bacchus and Ariadne dish in the Love Collection marked by Paul Storr in 1817 (cat. no. 9). The trelliswork borders on these two dishes appear to be from the same moulds, suggesting that Rundell's had supplied the models to Storr in 1817.

In style, the central relief of Nike leading horses of a quadriga is quite unlike Stothard's relief on the matching dish, which was based on an engraving of an antique Roman cameo. The more severe, linear style of the Nike relief recalls John Flaxman's outline drawings and his early cameo-like designs for Wedgwood ceramics. However, the actual designer of this relief was probably the medal-engraver and cameo-carver Benedetto Pistrucci (1784-1855), to whom Oman tentatively ascribed the design for the central scene of another sideboard dish by Philip Rundell of 1822.[1] Rundell's regularly commissioned and supplied medals, and presumably had many dealings with Pistrucci, the leading medallist of his day and officially Chief Medallist to the King. Pistrucci's autobiography records that he designed a large medal of George IV "as speculation for Messrs. Rundell and Bridge." He also supplied other firms with designs for medals, including one to the retailer Hamlet for a medal of the Duke of York.[2]

fig. 39 Benedetto Pistrucci, The Waterloo Medal, 5½ in. (13.5cm.) diameter. *Courtesy Spink.*

The central figure of Nike and the outer two horses on the Love dish closely follow but are reversed from those on Pistrucci's well known Great Waterloo Medal (fig. 39). Pistrucci began the designs for this medal, which was to be struck in gold for presentation to the allied sovereigns, in 1816, but the dies were not completed until 1849.[3] Pistrucci's competitor for the Waterloo Medal was John Flaxman, but Pistrucci, by refusing to make dies from another sculptor's designs, managed to win the commission.[4]

1. Charles Oman, *English Silversmiths' Work, Civil and Domestic*, London, 1965, fig. 207.
2. A Billings, *The Science of Gems, Jewels, Coins and Medals*, London, 1875, p. 207.
3. Laurence Brown, *A Catalogue of British Historical Medals, 1760-1960*, London, 1980, vol. I, pp. 209-212. The long delay in the production of this medal resulted from Pistrucci's disputes with the Mint Master over the position of Chief Engraver, which Pistrucci wanted and apparently deserved.
4. Graham Pollard, "Flaxman and Designs for Medals and Coins," in David Bindman, ed., *John Flaxman*, London, 1979, p. 135.

11. A PAIR OF GEORGE IV SAUCEBOATS

Maker's mark of Robert Garrard II
London, 1820
The liners with maker's mark of
Sebastian Crespel II

Height 9 ½ in. (24 cm.)
Weight 115 oz. (3,593 gr.)

Robert Garrard II based these sauceboats on examples from the well known "Marine Service" commissioned by Frederick, Prince of Wales in 1741-1744. The service, which remains in the Royal Collection, comprises a centerpiece, a set of four sauceboats, and various models of salt cellars, most marked by Nicholas Sprimont, in a French-inspired rococo style employing marine motifs. The present sauceboats are exact copies of Sprimont's examples of 1743-1744 (fig. 40). [1] The figures surmounting the sterns of these sauceboats have in the past been identified as Venus and Adonis, but they more likely represent a water nymph and her companion.

A number of English silversmiths copied elements of the "Marine Service," most notably James Young and Robert Hennell, who made a centerpiece, sauceboats matching the present examples, and salts for Charles Manners, 4th Duke of Rutland, in 1780. [2] The handles on the Rutland sauceboats and those on the present examples closely follow the Sprimont originals, while some later versions by Garrard employ different figures. The pair by Garrard of 1824 in the Gans Collection have figural handles formerly thought to be formed as Jupiter and Hebe, but more probably depicting another water nymph and her companion. [3]

An idea of the original cost of these sauceboats is given in the Garrard ledgers, where a set of eight with ladles were charged to the Earl of Harborough on 13 February 1819 as follows:

8 finely chased sauceboats with figure handles supported by dolphins and rock work. 465ozs 10dwts £519 5s. [4]

fig. 40 One of four George II silver sauceboats from the "Marine Service" made for Frederick, Prince of Wales, maker's mark of Nicholas Sprimont, London, 1743-1744, 9 in. (23 cm.) high. *The Royal Collection © 1997, Her Majesty Queen Elizabeth II.*

1. The centerpiece in the Marine Service is marked by Paul Crespin but attributed to Sprimont and dated 1741. One sauceboat from the set of four matching this boat-shaped model is illustrated in E.A. Jones, *The Gold and Silver of Windsor Castle,* Letchworth, 1911, pl.I. Two are illustrated in *Rococo: Art and Design in Hogarth's England*, London, 1984, G17, p.114, and another in Arthur Grimwade, *Rococo Silver,* London, 1974, fig.33A, pp.31-32. The salt cellars in the Marine service comprise a pair formed as crabs marked by Sprimont and dated 1743, and a pair formed as lobsters marked by Sprimont and dated 1743. Two pairs of small dishes on triton or dragon stems, unmarked, have recently been identified as sweetmeat dishes intended to fit into the main centerpiece. One of the crab-form salts is illustrated in Grimwade, *op. cit.,* fig.378.
2. The Rutland pieces were sold on behalf of the 10th Duke of Rutland, Christie's London, 16 January 1944, lots 44-47 (incorrectly dated 1820). The boat-shaped sauceboats and the salts with triton stems are illustrated by Michael Clayton, *The Collector's Dictionary of Silver and Gold of Great Britain and North America,* London, 1971 ed., fig. 485.
3. Illustrated in Joseph Bliss, *The Jerome and Rita Gans Collection of English Silver on Loan to the Virginia Museum of Fine Arts,* n.d., cat. no. 68, pp.196-197. These sauceboats were also lent to the exhibition, *Royal Goldsmiths: The Garrard Heritage,* London 1991, and are illustrated in the catalogue of the same title, pp.66. A further set of four by Garrard of 1819 and 1820, engraved with a crest thought to be that of Carrington, were sold at Sotheby's, New York, 7April 1987, lot 113.
4. Garrard Ledgers, Victoria and Albert Museum, GL2, p.101.

12. THE DUKE OF YORK'S CENTERPIECE: A GEORGE IV NINE-LIGHT CANDELABRUM FORMED AS HERCULES ATTACKING THE HYDRA

Maker's mark of Edward Farrell
London, 1824
The nozzles 1825
Retailed by Kensington Lewis

Height 35in. (89cm.)
Weight 1,144oz. (32,432gr.)

PROVENANCE
H.R.H. Prince Frederick Augustus, Duke of York and Albany, K.G., P.C., G.C.B (1763-1827), second son of George III
The Magnificent Silver and Silver-Gilt Plate of His Royal Highness, The Duke of York, Deceased, Christie's, London, March 19-22, 1827, first day's sale lot 62
Sir Clive Milnes Coates, Bt., (in whose family the centerpiece had been since the Duke of York's sale), Christie's, London, 18 October 1967, lot 59.

LITERATURE
Christie's Review of the Season, 1967-1968, London, 1968, pp. 150-151
Arthur Grimwade, "Two Great Royal Silver Sales," *Christie's Review of the Season,* London, 1975, pp. 196-197
John Culme, "Kensington Lewis: a Nineteenth-Century Businessman," *Connoisseur,* September 1975, pp. 31 and 36
John Culme, *Nineteenth-Century Silver,* London, 1977, pp. 73-74
Michael Clayton, *Christie's Pictorial History of English and American Silver,* Oxford, 1985, fig.7, p. 249

EXHIBITED
Temple Newsam, "Domestic Silver from Yorkshire Houses," 1959

One of the most important pieces of silver from the first half of the 19th century, the Duke of York's centerpiece can justifiably be claimed to be Edward Farrell's masterpiece. Based on a variety of historical design sources, it is the ultimate example of eclecticism in English silver design. It was supplied to the Duke of York, among much other silver-gilt and silver, by Kensington Lewis, an influential antiquarian and for a short time one of the leading silver retailers in London. The extraordinary group of silver made for the Duke of York by Edward Farrell under the direction of Kensington Lewis was undoubtedly the most innovative silver of its time, and anticipates the full-blown historicism of the mid-19th century. An able salesman, Lewis channeled the Duke's profligate spending toward an obscure but extremely talented silversmith capable of creating new designs from a variety of art historical sources. It was this phenomenal collaboration of patron, retailer, and craftsman which resulted in these distinctive and extravagant objects, five of which are now in the Love Collection.

fig. 41 Andrea del Verrocchio, Figure of the Executioner from the Beheading of St. John the Baptist, Florence, 1478-1483, a silver relief plaque from a festival altar. *Museo dell'Opera del Duomo, Florence.*

Given that the Duke of York was best known as Commander-in-Chief of the Army, it is likely that Hercules was chosen as the subject of this centerpiece to symbolize that important office. In this light, the Hydra can be seen as representing the enemies of England. The image of Hercules Slaying the Hydra has been used for centuries to imply military might as well as victory over the vices. Henry IV of France, for example, was portrayed at least twice as Hercules the Conqueror, with the slain hydra at his feet (fig. 42). [1] In Georgian England,

fig. 42 Leonard Gaultier, Portrait of Henry IV as Hercules Slaying the Hydra, engraving, 1602. *Bibliothèque Nationale de France, Paris.*

John Flaxman had used Hercules and the Hydra as the central relief on his silver "Trafalgar Vase" of 1805, inscribed "Britannia Triumphant/ Britons Strike Home." [2] Although Lewis and Farrell included the traditional attributes of Hercules in this sculptural group, such as the crab sent by Hera to aid the Hydra and Hercules's ally Iolaus, the actual composition of the model seems to be their own invention, a combination of various design sources. Ubaldo Vitali has found that Farrell's figure of Hercules is based on a painting of the same subject by Ciro Ferri, which was popularised in engravings of the 17th century. [3] This distinctive pose, with right knee raised and head looking over the left shoulder, derives in turn from Michelangelo's figure of Charon in the Sistine Chapel. Andrew Butterfield has identified the figure of Iolaus as modelled after Verrochio's figure of the Executioner in a silver plaque of the Beheading of St. John the Baptist, found on an altar made for the Duomo in Florence around 1480 (fig. 41). [4] Given the fame of this altarpiece, which is cited in Vasari's *Lives,* it is likely that many engravings were made from it as well. The modeller of this centerpiece, like most sculptors working in England in this period, probably trained in Italy and therefore would have been familiar with these Renaissance images. It is the combining of the two figures, lifted entirely out of their original contexts and from two different centuries, which is so typical of Lewis's highly eclectic style.

The Duke of York was born Prince Frederick Augustus, second son of King George III and younger brother of George Augustus, later George IV. In 1780, at the age of seventeen, he was made Colonel in the Royal Army, beginning his lifelong military career. The following year he left England for Hanover, travelling extensively in Europe to study both French and German language as well as the military tactics of the Austrian and Prussian armies. In 1794, he was created Duke of York and Albany. At the age of 28, he dutifully married Princess Frederica, eldest daughter of Friedrich Wilhelm II, King of Prussia, although they separated fairly shortly thereafter. At the time of his marriage in 1791 he was said to have had the enormous annual income of £70,000.

Following the outbreak of the war with France in 1793, the Duke fought in the Flanders campaigns, was promoted to Field Marshall in 1795, and became Commander-in-Chief of the Army three years later. In 1809 he was accused of corruption on account of the practices of his mistress Mary Ann Clarke, who profited from her intimacy with the Commander-in-Chief by selling promotions to officers. The scandal forced him to resign for two years, but he was reinstated in 1811.

On the death of George III, the Duke of York's older brother, to whom he was very close, became King George IV and he, heir to the throne. Both brothers bought enormous quantities of silver, both antique and modern, mostly from Rundell's and were together the most important collectors of silver in England. Their antiquarian tastes were shared to a lesser extent by two of their younger brothers, the Dukes of Cambridge and Sussex. George IV and other Royal Dukes, however, did not apparently patronize Kensington Lewis, so these monumental works by Farrell can be credited to the patronage of the Duke of York alone.

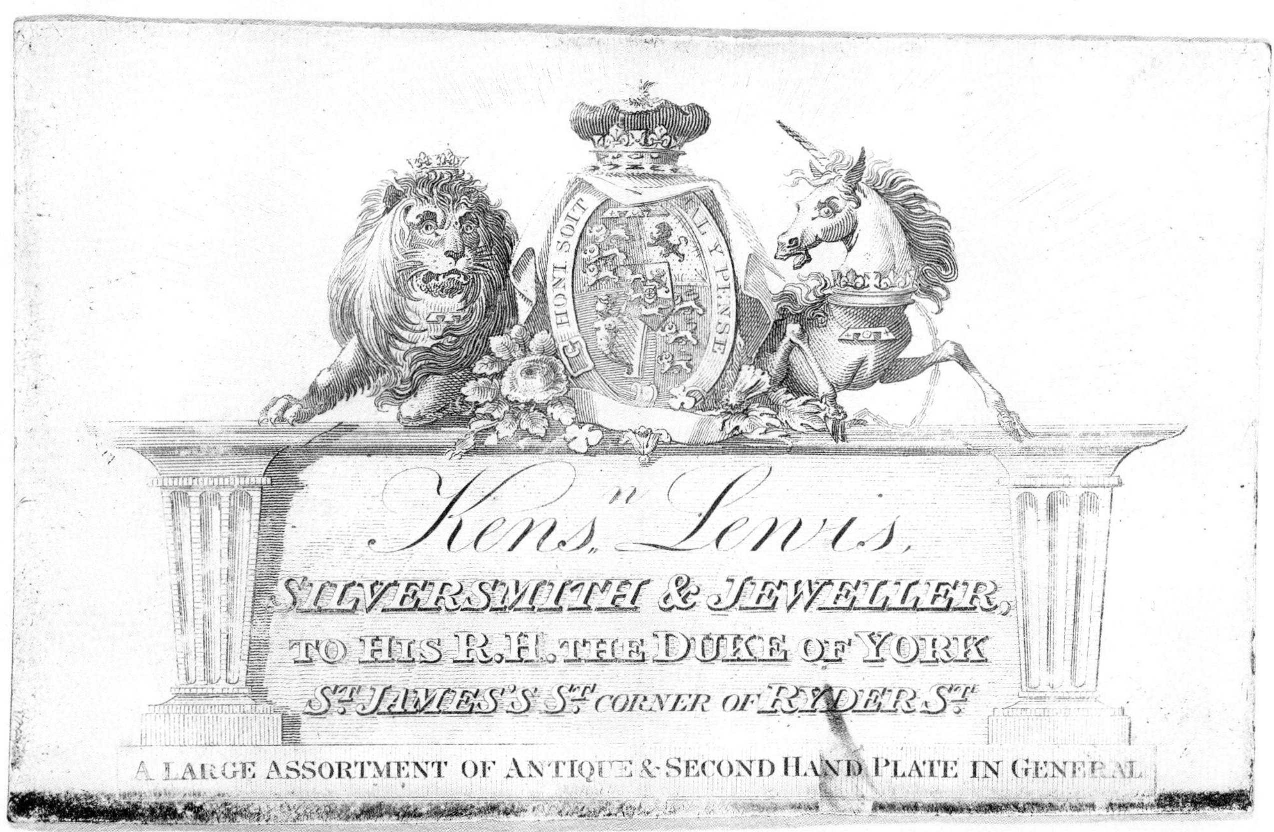

fig. 43 Trade Card of Kensington Lewis, advertising "a Large Assortment of Antique & Second Hand Plate in General," engraving, 1822-1827. *Copyright © The British Museum.*

The Duke of York died in 1827 leaving debts somewhere between £200,000 and £500,000—the imprecise figure being perhaps an indication of just how chaotic the Duke's financial affairs were at the time of his death. In order to try to satisfy these huge debts, his executors took the unprecedented step of selling a Royal collection by public auction. The Duke of York's silver was offered at Christie's in a four-day sale starting on March 19th 1827. Viewing of the silver was by ticket and a copy of the catalogue admitted a prospective buyer to the auction itself. At the outset of the sale, James Christie II eulogised the late Duke and was "warmly applauded by the company." No doubt his announcement that the sale "had not a single reserve" was equally well received. [5]

The Hercules Centerpiece took pride of place in the sale catalogue appearing with "that grand work of art, THE SHIELD OF ACHILLES" and a dessert-service on the title page of the catalogue. It was there described as:

A GRAND CANDELABRUM
COMPOSED OF A GROUP OF
HERCULES DESTROYING THE HYDRA

Of Silver Gilt, weighing upwards of One Thousand ounces, made by Mr. Lewis

Lot 62 in the first day's sale has the following description under the general heading of:

MASSIVE SILVER GILT PLATE

A MAGNIFICENT CANDELABRUM, or group, for the centre of table, *(made by Lewis)* representing HERCULES ATTACKING the HYDRA, and surrounded by its nine heads, which bear as many nozzles for lights. Iolaus, the companion of Hercules, is searing a neck of the monster below. The group is supported on a mass of rock work, about the base of which are various reptiles.

Weight of the whole, 1144 oz. 5dwts.

> THIS VERY GRAND and MASSIVE PIECE of PLATE, rests upon a base of brass, forming the lower part of the rock, and is supported upon brass castors, to facilitate the placing it in the centre of the table. *Also, a very strong mahogany chest or cabinet, brass bound, to contain the candelabrum.*

The prices for the sale as a whole, and the centerpiece in particular, were not good. According to one newspaper, "the general opinion was, that the articles did not bring near so much as they were worth intrinsically, and certainly not as much as they cost, especially the splendid massive silver plate." The centerpiece was knocked down for £343/5/6, or 6s an ounce—something in the region of a quarter of its original purchase price. [6] Indeed, the newspaper records that "after Mr. Christie had dwelt a considerable time at the bidding, there was a murmour ran round the room of 'How cheap!' when the hammer fell. Mr. Christie said that the candelabrum was purchased by the late illustrious owner for the new Palace, which it pleased Providence that he was never to inhabit. 'Notwithstanding I feel sorry for the sacrifice which has been made in this article,' said Mr. Christie, 'I feel greater grief that the workmanship of the artist is valued so low. The design is most beautiful, and there exists only another like it in England.' " [7] The total for the four-day sale of the silver was £22,438/10s while the Duke's arms and armour collection and furniture brought in a further £15,000 or so.

Apart from the Hercules centerpiece, the catalogue included a number of other items described as being "by Lewis." In addition, there are several more items of silver that, from their descriptions alone, can confidently be attributed to Farrell, and were presumably supplied by Lewis. The working relationship of the two has been studied by John Culme in his article on Kensington Lewis published in 1975. [8] Culme was able to identify three items that were made by Farrell for Kensington Lewis who sold them to the Duke of York: the present Hercules centerpiece, a massive pair of ewers with the arms of France, and a large pair of salvers. [9] Since that date, a number of items made by Farrell for the Duke of York have come to light. [10] The Love Collection contributes four more pieces to this group: the pair of large six-light Neptune candelabra (cat. no. 13), the smaller pair of four-light candelabra with Triton and Nereid stems (cat. no. 14), a single candelabrum with Triton stem (not included in the current exhibition), and the ewer altered by Farrell (cat. no. 15), all of which can be identified in the 1827 sale.

Lewis Kensington Solomon (c. 1790-1854) was the son of Samuel Solomon, a retired silversmith dealing in bullion and military accessories. In 1811 or before, he changed his name to Kensington Lewis. [11] He first appears in the silver world at the sale at Christie's London on May 24-25, 1816 of "Ancient Massive Plate, Pictures etc" from the estate of the 11th Duke of Norfolk, where he purchased two lots which were in all probability 17th century European in origin. Far from inexpensive, these purchases clearly indicate Lewis's serious interest in antique silver. Presumably under Lewis's direction, Edward Farrell drew on a range of 16th, 17th and 18th century decorative elements and forms to produce the most innovative and distinctive silver of the period.

At what point Lewis started employing Farrell is difficult to ascertain. The monteith of 1820 in the Gilbert Collection is the earliest known piece that is both marked by Farrell and stamped with Lewis's signature (fig. 45). [12] If we assume that Farrell's use of antique styles was encouraged by Lewis, the connection may go back to around 1816 (see cat. no. 17 for a tankard by Farrell dated 1816 in German late 17th-century taste). Although not signed bt Lewis, a set of twelve salt cellars of 1817 can be identified in the Duke of York's sale (p. 74). By 1822, Lewis had opened a retail shop on 22 St. James's Street, on the corner of Ryder Street, a block away from both St. James's Palace and from Christie's (fig. 43). Within a short time, he was being patronized by the Duke of York. This important client coupled with Lewis's genius for self-promotion allowed him by 1825 to open a second retail shop in the newly built Regent Street. Unfortunately for Lewis, the death of the Duke of York seems to have led to a rapid decline in his business. Not only did he lose his most important client, but the Duke owed him over £2,300, a debt that took the estate eighteen years to repay. In addition, the bad publicity surrounding the prices fetched at the Duke of York's estate auction—in many cases a quarter or less than those originally charged by Lewis—can hardly have helped his reputation. After a series of bad real estate investments and a short time in debtor's prison, he died in 1854. [13]

Relatively little is known of Edward Farrell. He was born sometime between 1775 and 1781. It is likely that from 1801, when he was first recorded living in London, until 1813, when he entered his first mark at Goldsmiths' Hall, he was an outworker for some other workshop. At some point over the next few years, he seems to have started to work for Lewis. From then until the Duke's death was a time of great financial success for Lewis and artistic experimentation and triumph for Farrell. Of the eighty different items marked by Farrell, close to three quarters were made prior to 1827, although he lived until 1850. The decline in variety and artistic creativity of Farrell's work parallels the apparent break-up of the business connection between Farrell and Lewis sometime in the mid-1830s.

1. We are grateful to Ubaldo Vitali for recognizing the relevance of the Hercules and Hydra subject and for the reference to Henry IV.
2. Illustrated in David Bindman, ed., *John Flaxman*, London, 1979, pl. I. The Trafalgar Vase was one of a series of 66 vases to the same design commissioned by Lloyd's Patriotic Fund from 1804-1809.
3. Giovanni Bonacina engraved a print after Ciro Ferri's Hercules around 1650.
4. We are indebted to Andrew Butterfield for identifying the design source, which is in discussed in his forthcoming monograph, *The Sculptures of Andrea del Verrocchio*, New Haven and London, 1997.
5. Newspaper account of the Duke of York's sale quoted by W. Roberts, *Memorials of Christie's*, London, 1897, vol. I, pp.113-115.
6. John Culme, "Kensington Lewis: A Nineteenth-Century Businessman," *Connoisseur*, September, 1975, p.36.
7. Roberts, *op. cit.*, p.115
8. Culme, *op. cit.*, pp. 26-41.
9. The ewers sold at Sotheby's, New York, 16-17 December 1982, lot 541 (ex Duke of York's sale, March 19, lots 66 and 67); the salvers sold at Christie's, London, 15 June 1983 lot 213 (ex Duke of York's sale, March 19, lots 69 and 70). The latter are now in the Al-Tajir Collection (see exhibition catalogue, *The Glory of the Goldsmith*, London, 1989, no. 154)
10. These are:
    a) A monteith by Farrell, 1820, stamped with Lewis's signature, sold at Sotheby's, London, 15 June 1978, lot 169 (ex Duke of York's sale, 19 March 1827, lot 71), now in the Gilbert collection (see Timothy Schroder, *The Gilbert Collection of Gold and Silver*, Los Angeles, 1988, no 117).
    b) A pair of pilgrim bottles by Farrell, 1825, inset with earlier plaques, engraved with the Duke of York's arms and stamped with Lewis's signature, sold at Christie's, London, 15 July 1975, lot 134, now also in the Gilbert Collection (Schroder, *op.cit.*, no. 122). These are not identifiable in the Duke of York's sale and may have been a gift before his death to William Henry Vane, 1st Marquess and 4th Duke of Cleveland whose arms they also bear.
    c) Two soup-tureens by Farrell, 1823, one signed Lewis, engraved with the Duke of York's arms, sold at Christie's, New York, 15 October 1985, lots 199 and 200 (ex Duke of York's sale March 19, 1827, either lots 21 or 22 and either lots 27 or 28 respectively)
    d) Three vegetable-dishes and covers by Farrell, 1823, stamped with Lewis's signature, sold Christie's, New York, 27 October 1992, lot 231 (ex Duke of York's sale, either part of lots 53 or 54)
    e) A cruet-frame by Farrell, 1825, engraved with the Duke of York's arms, sold at Christie's, New York, 17 April 1996, lot 86 (ex Duke of York's sale, 21 March 1827, lot 40)
    f) A muffin-dish and cover by Farrell, 1818, similarly engraved, sold from the Meech Collection, Sotheby's, New York, 17 October 1995, lot 59 (ex Duke of York's sale, 19 March 1827, either lot 107 or 108)
    g) Two bowls after James I wood examples, by Farrell, 1824, sold at Christie's, London, 12 November 1980, lot 71 and at Sotheby's, London, 24 October 1985, lot 452 (ex Duke of York's sale, 19 March 1827, two of 34 sold as lots 79-82).
11. Culme, *op. cit.*, p.26
12. Timothy Schroder, *The Gilbert Collection of Gold and Silver*, Los Angeles, 1988, no.117.
13. For details of Lewis's life after the Duke of York's sale, see Culme, *op. cit.*, pp.37-41.

13. A PAIR OF GEORGE IV SIX-LIGHT CANDELABRA

With the maker's mark only of Edward Farrell
London, 1819-1826
Also struck with spurious marks for Paul Storr, London, 1828

Height 28in. (71 cm.)
a) Weight 381 oz. (11,870 gr.)
b) Weight 389 oz. (12,100 gr.)

PROVENANCE
H.R.H. Prince Frederick, Duke of York and Albany, K.G., P.C., G.C.B. (1763-1827), second son of George III
The Magnificent Silver and Silver-Gilt Plate of His Royal Highness, The Duke of York, Deceased, Christie's, London, 19-22 March 1827, first day's sale lots 64 and 65

The erasure of the original hallmarks makes accurate dating of these candelabra impossible. [1] While it is likely that they were made ensuite with Farrell's candelabrum centerpiece for the Duke of York of 1824 (cat. no. 12), the existence of a similar slightly larger candelabrum by Farrell dated 1819 raises the possibility that these candelabra could have been made earlier (fig. 44). [2]

The weights and size of the current examples however leave little doubt that they are indeed the ones listed in the Duke of York's sale. The catalogue descriptions for lot 63, a similar candelabrum with a seahorse instead of a dolphin, and the subsequent two lots, which describe the present pair, appear as follows:

fig. 44 Regency silver six-light candelabrum, maker's mark of Edward Farrell, London, 1819, 30 in. (76 cm.) high. *Christie's photograph.*

MASSIVE SILVER GILT PLATE

Lot 63 A SUPERB CANDELABRUM, by ditto [i.e. Lewis], about 34 inches high composed of a figure of NEPTUNE, one knee supported upon a sea horse, but standing upon a rock covered with marine productions. The right arm supports a shell upon his head, from which springs a hydra with five necks, bearing five sconces for lights, the whole producing a truly splendid effect. Weight of the candelabrum, 542 oz. 10dwts. Also a mahogany brass-bound case for ditto [£180/]

Lot 64 A SMALLER CANDELABRUM of nearly the same design, and nearly 28 inches high, but the figure of Neptune is supported by a dolphin: the hydra is disposed in branches to bear six lights: weight 388 oz. 10dwts. [£135/14/6]

Lot 65 THE COMPANION CANDELABRUM. Weight, 395 oz. 10dwts. [£133/6]

1. The original hallmarks were deliberately removed when the spurious Storr marks were added, but Farrell's maker's marks beneath each base were overlooked and fortunately survive. The marks on the exterior are clearly false and were presumably applied sometime this century to make the candelabra appear to be by Paul Storr, a better known and more commerciably valuable maker than Farrell.
2. The related candelabrum of 1819 was sold at Christie's, New York, 27 September 1978, lot 213. It was reputedly from the collection of the Late Evalyn Walsh MacLean and one of five similar examples in poor condition, all sold as part of her estate at the Meredith Galleries, Washington, D.C., in 1948. This candelabrum is of the same design as described in lot 63 in the Duke of York's sale, but is of a different weight and size.

14. A PAIR OF REGENCY FOUR-LIGHT CANDELABRA

Maker's mark of Paul Storr
London, 1819

Height 21in. (53cm.)
a) weight 216 oz. (6718 gr.)
b) weight 220 oz. (6842 gr.)

PROVENANCE
H.R.H. Prince Frederick Augustus, Duke of York and Albany, K.G., P.C., G.C.B. (1763-1827), second son of George III
The Magnificent Silver and Silver-Gilt Plate of His Royal Highness, The Duke of York, Deceased, Christie's, London, 19-22 March, 1827, first day's sale a) lot 77, b) lot 78

These candelabra raise a number of questions both concerning their identification in the Duke of York's sale and also about the appearance of Storr's mark on what appear to be typical examples of Farrell's work. In addition to these candelabra, there are in the Love Collection two others of similar form, one by Edward Farrell, 1818, and a matching candelabrum which appears to be a later casting from it.

In the Duke of York's sale the relevant candelabra are described under:

MASSIVE SILVER-GILT PLATE

Lot 75 A candelabrum, twenty-one inches high representing a triton seated upon a sea-horse, with reptiles and marine productions; upon the head of the figure is a shell, from which spring the heads of the hydra, forming branches for four lights, weight 213 oz
[£92/6/8]

Lot 76 A ditto, with a sea-nymph on a sea-horse, the companion; weight 209 oz. 10 dwts.
[£91/10/17]

Lot 77 A ditto, with a triton upon a dolphin, in other respects similar; weight 218 oz. 10 dwts.
[£91/5]

Lot 78 A ditto, with a sea-nymph upon a dolphin, the companion; weight 222 oz. 10 dwts.
[£95/5]

The closeness of the current weights of the present candelabra to those in the catalogue strongly suggest that they are indeed lots 77 and 78. The third candelabrum by Farrell in the Love Collection resembles the description for lot 75, but features a dolphin rather than a sea-horse, and therefore cannot be considered to be from the Duke of York's collection. [1]

Regarding the appearance of Paul Storr's mark on these typically Farrell models, one possible explanation is that Farrell supplied Storr with the moulds for casting. The 1818 Farrell example in the Love Collection indicates the the model was certainly in existence when Storr made the present examples. This period seems to have been a busy one for Farrell, with growing demands from Kensington Lewis on behalf of the Duke of York and others. It may simply be that in order to cope with this increased demand, Farrell had to turn to the workshop of Paul Storr in this instance.

1. The 1818 Farrell example currently weighs 204 ozs. and is in poor condition.

15. A GEORGE III EWER

Maker's mark of Thomas Holland II
London, 1807
One sword with addition marks for 1823,
Later chasing and applied additions attributed to Edward Farrell, circa 1823

Height 13 ¾ in. (34.9 cm.)
Weight 87 oz. (2,710gr.)

Engraved with the Royal arms and badge of The Duke of York. Also engraved with the monogram AGBC for Angela Georgina, Baroness Burdett-Coutts.

PROVENANCE
H.R.H. Prince Frederick Augustus, Duke of York and Albany, K.G., P.C., G.C.B (1763-1827), second son of George III
The Magnificent Silver and Silver-Gilt Plate of His Royal Highness the Duke of York, Deceased, Christie's, London, 19-22 March 1827, first day's sale lot 73
Angela Georgina, Baroness Burdett-Coutts (1814-1906)
Anonymous sale, Sotheby's, London, 22 June 1967, lot 57

LITERATURE
Vanessa Brett, *The Sotheby's Directory of Silver*, London, 1986, p. 246, no. 1107

This extremely interesting ewer is one of at least seven recorded examples by Holland with certain features in common. [1] All are hallmarked for the year 1807 and each has an identical, very distinctive handle formed as a male caryatid with floral wreaths around his head and waist. With the exception of the present example, all have at the shoulder a cast band incorporating two demi-putti flanking a lyre. The short cast spout with scroll border and floral swag above a female mask is similar on all the examples. It is possible that the rococo revival bases on four of these ewers are by Holland, whose few surviving pieces display unusual features and a somewhat awkward mixture of styles. [2] It is also possible that these elaborate bases are replacements by Edward Farrell.

There is no doubt, however, that Farrell is the author of the battle scenes around the body of the present example. While only one sword is marked with the addition mark for 1823, the central equestrian figure, said to be Alexander, and the figures surrounding him in battle on both sides of the ewer are identical to those on either side of Farrell's well-known monteith of 1820 made for the Duke of York (fig. 45). [3] The scenes are so similar that the present ewer and its mate, now missing, must originally have flanked the monteith. The three pieces, together with a ladle for the monteith, were in fact consecutive lots in the Duke of York's sale. The pair of ewers is described in the catalogue under:

MASSIVE SILVER GILT PLATE

Lot 73 A PRAEFERICULUM, the lip formed of the stem of a vine with fruit, the handle, a terminal recurved: round the bowl of the vessel is represented one of the battles of Alexander, in superb chasing; the stem and foot formed of very rich chasing and scroll work. 13½ inches high, to the top of the handle weight 87oz 5dwt
[£69/16]

Lot 74 A DITTO, the Companion, weight 81 oz
[£70]

Following the Duke of York's sale, the ewer eventually passed into the collection of Angela Burdett-Coutts, daughter of Sir Francis Burdett, 5th Bt., and his wife Sophia, whose father was the immensely wealthy banker Thomas Coutts. In 1815, Thomas Coutts had married at the age of 81 the actress Harriet Mellon, who was less than half his age. On his death seven years later she inherited his huge fortune. *The Morning Post* reported that "sometime previous to his death he settled on Mrs. C. the sum of £600,000 with the house in Stratton-street, all the plate, linen, & c.—the service of plate is said to be the most valuable in any of the country—together with the house in Highgate and all its appurtenances . . . the whole makes her the richest

widow in the Kingdom." She married secondly in 1827 William, 9th Duke of St. Albans, 20 years her junior. On her death in 1837, she left much of her fortune and her silver to her youngest step-granddaughter Angela Georgina Burdett who assumed the additional surname of Coutts.

Contemporary newspaper accounts pointed out that the 23-year-old Angela Burdett-Coutts had inherited the equivalent of thirteen tons of gold. She used her wealth to add to her inherited art collection and to support numerous charities. Her philanthropic activities were eventually rewarded by Queen Victoria who created her a Baroness in 1871. She married in 1881 the American William Bartlett, the younger son of Ellis Bartlett of Plymouth, Massachusetts. He took the Burdett-Coutts name in place of his own and became M.P. for Westminster in 1885. She died in 1906 and was buried in Westminster Abbey. Much of her silver was kept in storage until 1914 when the Coutts heirlooms were mostly dispersed at Christie's, although the present ewer does not appear in that catalogue. [4]

1. In addition to the present example, originally one of a pair, there appear to be at least six recorded ewers by Thomas Holland of similar form and hallmarked in 1807:
a) a silver-gilt pair engraved with the arms of the 5th Baron Aylmer (1775-1850), 14 ¼ in. (36.2 cm.) high, weight for pair 168 oz. (5,224 gr.), sold at Sotheby's, London, 26 February 1976 lot 186, illustrated in Vanessa Brett, *The Sotheby's Directory of Silver*, London, 1986, no. 1108.
b) a single example (not gilt), engraved with the arms of Bolton impaling Littledale 13 ¾ in. (34.9 cm.) high, weight 60 oz. 2 dwt. (1,869 gr.), sold at Sotheby's, London, 17 May 1973, lot 49, illustrated in Brett, *op.cit.*, no. 1109.
c) The above ewer may be the same as, or a pair to, another similarly engraved and sold at Sotheby's, New York, 15 December 1983, lot 116. (the height at 14 ⅛ in. (35.8 cm.) and weight at 59oz. 15dwt. (1,858 gr.) varies very slightly from the above example).
d) a pair (not gilt) engraved with the arms of the 4th Baron Monson (b.1785), 14 ¼in. (36.2 cm.) high, weight for pair 148 oz. 10dwt. (4,618 gr.), sold at Sotheby's, London, 15 October 1970, lot 57, illustrated in Brett, *op. cit.*, no. 1110.
e) A silver-gilt example with later applied plaque and inscription dated 1822, 14 ⅛in. (35.8 cm.) high, weight 79 oz. (2,457 gr.), sold at Sotheby's, New York, 21 April 1983, lot 270.

2. See, for example, the epergne by Holland of 1803 with Egyptian bust supports and branches formed as cornucopiae entwined with serpents, sold at Sotheby's, New York, 13 April 1988, lot 221.
3. The Duke of York's sale, Christie's, London, 19 March 1827, lot 71, to Kensington Lewis. Sold anonymously, Sotheby's, London, 15 June 1978, lot 169. Illustrated in Brett, *op. cit.*, p.271, no. 1243. It is now in the Gilbert Collection and illustrated and described by Timothy Schroder, *The Gilbert Collection of Gold and Silver*, Los Angeles, 1988, pp. 434-437, no. 117.
4. For further details on the Duchess of St. Albans and Angela Burdett-Coutts see Christie's, New York, 18 October 1995, lot 315 and Christie's, New York, 17 April, 1996, lot 112.

fig. 45 George IV silver-gilt monteith, maker's mark of Edward Farrell, London, 1820, stamped *LEWIS SILVERSMITH TO H.R.H. THE DUKE OF YORK, ST. JAMES'S ST.*, 15 ⅜ in. (39 cm.) high. *The Rosalinde and Arthur Gilbert Collection. Photograph Los Angeles Museum of Art.*

16. A SET OF TWELVE REGENCY SALT CELLARS WITH TWELVE SALT SPOONS

Maker's mark of Edward Farrell
London, 1817
Presumably retailed by Kensington Lewis

Height 6 ½in. (16.5 cm.)
Weight 378oz. (10,788gr.)
Weight of spoons 29oz. (826gr.)

These superb salt cellars with bases formed as Neptune, Amphitrite, Tritons, and Nereids are early examples of Edward Farrell's work under the direction of retailer and antiquarian, Kensington Lewis. They are important objects in both Lewis's and Farrell's career, not only in their early date, but also in their subject matter, which may have been inspired by a prototype from the 11th Duke of Norfolk's collection of European antique silver. Kensington Lewis's first known appearance in the silver marketplace was at the Duke of Norfolk's sale of 1816 at Christie's, where he purchased two lots, one of which was a silver-gilt cup and salver decorated with "figures of marine dieties" and "sea nymphs and tritons in relief." [1]

The design of these salt cellars was evidently a successful one for Lewis, as he also engaged Farrell in the same year to make an identical set for the Duke of York, who over the next nine years became the collaborators' most important patron (cat. no. 12). The Duke of York's salts of this model, later owned by Victor Rothschild, are the earliest known pieces of silver made by Farrell for Lewis in the Duke of York's auction, where they are described as follows:

SUPERB VESSELS FOR THE TABLE
AND SIDEBOARD, OF SILVER GILT PLATE

71 A set of six superb salt cellars, composed of Tritons and Nymphs, mounted on sea horses, and bearing each a shell for salt; weight 180 oz
[The weight is amended in the auctioneer's book to 164 oz. and they sold for £79/5/4]

72 Six ditto spoons, with chased vines with fruit and figures; weight 10oz. 10dwts.
[The weight is amended in the auctioneer's book to 13 oz. and they sold for £6/16/6]

73 A set of six ditto, composed of Tritons and Nymphs on Dolphins; weight 160 oz.
[Amended weight 136oz. -sold for £68]

74 Six salt spoons, with chased vines, fruit, and figures, ditto; weight, 10oz. 10dwts
[Amended weight 10 oz. 10dwts.-sold for £6/16/6][2]

Another set of eight salt cellars of this model dated 1820, with eight spoons of 1817, are in the collection of Burghley House. [3] A further set of four salts of 1818 has recently come to light. [4]

The Duke of York also purchased twelve more salt cellars from Lewis, each described as a shell "with Tritons forming the support and handle, a figure of a tortoise furnishes the plinth." Although of a different model, these salts were accompanied by spoons identical to the present examples. [5]

1. As quoted in John Culme, "Kensington Lewis: a Nineteenth-Century Businessman," *Connoisseur*, September 1975, p.26.
2. The Magnificent Silver and Silver-Gilt Plate of His Royal Highness, The Duke of York, Deceased, Christie's, London, 19-22 March 1827, second day's sale, lots 71-74. The weights of the Rothschild salts identify them as the Duke of York's set. They were sold in the sale of Victor Rothschild Esq., Sotheby's & Co., London, April 26, 1937, lot 23.
3. John Webster, *Burghley House: Silver Exhibition*, 1984, no.30, p.29.
4. Sold at Christie's, London, March 5, 1997, lot 97.
5. The Duke of York's sale, lots 85 and 86; the spoons, lots 87 and 88. A pair of this model with tortoise base by Farrell, dated 1825, is illustrated in Michael Clayton, *Christie's Pictorial History of English and American Silver*, Oxford, 1985, fig.2, p.272.

17. A REGENCY TANKARD

Maker's mark of Edward Farrell
London, 1816

Height 11 ¼in. (28.5 cm.)
Weight 121 oz. (3,768 gm.)

PROVENANCE
The Trustees of the Cooper-Mullen Trust, Christie's, London, 1 July 1970, lot 45

LITERATURE
John Culme, "Kensington Lewis: A Nineteenth-Century Businessman," *Connoisseur*, September 1975, fig.3, p.28

Michael Clayton, *Christie's Pictorial History of English and American Silver,* Oxford, 1985, fig.7, p.269

This and the other tankard in the Love Collection (cat. no. 18) exemplify Farrell's earliest and most eclectic work. Based presumably on a late 17th-century German tankard, the decoration incorporates both neo-classical and baroque elements. The relief decorated body depicts the sacrifice of Iphigenia at Aulis, and the cover is chased in high relief with an equestrian scene.

Farrell's retailer, Kensington Lewis, undoubtedly supplied Farrell with the antique prototypes for such historicist works. At the 11th Duke of Norfolk's sale at Christie's in May 1816, Kensington Lewis bought "A NOBLE TANKARD, silver-gilt, with large compartment, on each side, the one comprising a feast of the Gods, in exquisite bas-relief, the other Apollo and Diana slaying the children of Niobe; on the lid is represented Alexander visiting the Tent of Darius; the handle fashioned as a syren-115oz." [1] The recent re-appearance at auction of a Farrell tankard very similar to the present example, but hall-marked a year earlier, indicates that Farrell was producing tankards in the 17th century German manner prior to Lewis's purchase at the Duke of Norfolk's sale. [2]

It should be noted that both Farrell's tankard of 1815 and the present example of 1816 have as their handles an unusual Bacchic herm figure. A somewhat similar handle with floral wreath around his stomach appears on another tankard of 1815, this time by Samuel Whitford, another maker working occasionally at this period in earlier styles. [3] All these handles are reminiscent of those found on the Duke of York's ewer by Thomas Holland of 1807, altered by Farrell in 1823 (cat. no. 15). This handle and those on six other ewers by Holland of 1807 were presumably supplied by a specialist handle maker over a number of years.

1. As quoted in John Culme, "Kensington Lewis: A Nineteenth-Century Businessman," *Connoisseur,* September 1975, p.27.
2. The Marquess of Exeter, Christie's London, 17 July 1959, lot 88, and Christie's, New York, 15 April 1997, lot 260.
3. Sir William Butlin, M.B.E. Christie's, London, 17 July 1968, lot 43, and Christie's, London, 25 March 1981, lot 150.

18. A REGENCY TANKARD

Maker's mark of Edward Farrell
London, 1817

Height 12in. (30.5 cm.)
Weight 185 oz. (5,768 gr.)

PROVENANCE
Sir William Butlin, M.B.E., Christie's, London, 17 July 1968, lot 41

This exceptionally heavy tankard, nearly fifty percent heavier than the other Farrell tankard in the Love Collection (cat. no. 17), must have been designed purely as an item of "display plate" rather than as a functional object. The quality of "massiveness" that Tatham strove for in the Camden dish (cat. no. 2) is apparent here, but the contrast between the riot of decoration on the tankard and the severe symmetrical ornament on the dish could not be more striking.

As with the other Farrell tankard in the collection, the cylindrical sleeve is cast and chased, this time with scenes of the Gods on Mount Olympus, over a plain cylindrical body. Unlike the other example, the massive base with dolphins and vines is bolted to the body. A Farrell tankard of 1815 and the two tankards in the Love Collection dated 1816 and 1817, show interesting developments in design. [1] All three have relief decorated sides and similar, rather awkward, domed covers. The 1815 tankard has a plain molded foot, while the 1816 example has added sculptural applications creating a heavier base. The present tankard of 1817, with its extremely sculptural handle joining the even heavier base, is arguably a more satisfactory design than either of its predecessors.

1. The 1815 example belonged to the Marquess of Exeter, and was sold at Christie's, London, 17 July 1959, lot 88, and again at Christie's, New York, 15 April 1997, lot 260.

19. A SET OF EIGHT GEORGE IV SALT CELLARS

Maker's mark of Edward Farrell
London, 1822, one salt-cellar unmarked

Length 4 ½in. (11.4cm.)
Weight 131 oz. (4,087 gr.)

The elaborate angular rockwork on the bases of these salts was used by Farrell on a number of pieces, most notably on the Hercules candelabrum (cat. no. 12). Comparisons can also be made with the rockwork bases marked by Philip Rundell in 1820, made for four earlier dessert dishes in the form of large shells supported by tritons and made by Paul Storr in 1812 for the Royal Collection. [1] The pen-and-wash drawings for the design of the dishes and stands is among those in a book of "Designs for Plate by John Flaxman etc" which are thought to be the work of Edward Hodges Baily (fig. 46). [2]

fig. 46 Pen-and-wash rendering for dessert stands on rockwork bases, attributed to Edward Hodges Baily, from Rundell's book of drawings titled "Designs for Plate by John Flaxman, etc." *Courtesy the Board of Trustees of the Victoria and Albert Museum.*

What has been described as the "marine rococo style" is thought to have derived in part from French designs of the mid 18th century. Liège-born silversmith Nicholas Sprimont made a number of pieces in this manner in London for Frederick, Prince of Wales in the 1740s. [3] Philip Rundell certainly had the opportunity to study Sprimont's pieces in the Royal Collection after Rundell and Bridge were appointed Goldsmith and Jeweller to the King in 1797, a position the firm, under a variety of names, retained until 1830. The firms of James Young, Robert Hennell and Robert Garrard are all known to have made direct copies of individual pieces in Frederick, Prince of Wales's celebrated "Marine Service" (cat. no. 11).

However, given the popularity of marine motifs from the 16th to the 18th centuries and the remarkably eclectic nature of early 19th century silver, the influence of Sprimont has probably been exaggerated. [4] In the case of the wine coolers in this style by Mortimer and Hunt, we know the inspiration came directly from a design by J-F-J Saly, a French artist of the 1740s who in turn may have been inspired by Renaissance models (cat. no. 22). It is also difficult to tell whether Rundell's influenced Farrell or vice versa. Certainly the appearance of a pair of four-light candelabra marked by Farrell (cat. no. 13) with a similar pair marked by Paul Storr (cat. no. 14) may indicate some degree of collaboration between Farrell and the Storr/Rundell partnership, particularly when a large order needed to be completed.

1. E. Alfred Jones, *The Gold and Silver of Windsor Castle,* Letchworth, 1911, p.180, pl.XCI, no.2.
2. Charles Oman, "A Problem of Artistic Responsibility: The Firm of Rundell, Bridge & Rundell," *Apollo*, January, 1966, p. 181.
3. *Ibid.*, p.182.
4. Giulio Romano, for example, drew a number of designs of shell-form salts on rockwork bases. See Beth L. Holman, ed., *Disegno: Italian Renaissance Designs for the Decorative Arts,* New York, 1997, figs. 24A, 24B, and 34, pp.107-108.

20. A GEORGE IV SALVER

Maker's mark of Edward Barton
London, 1824

Diameter 25 in. (63.5 cm.)
Weight 272 oz. (8463 gr.)

Engraved with the Royal Arms of Great Britain, as borne by the 1st Duke of Cambridge

PROVENANCE
Adolphus Frederick, 1st Duke of Cambridge (1771-1850), seventh son of George III
The 2nd Duke of Cambridge (1818-1904), Christie's, London, June 6, 1904, lot 202
Sir Weetman Dickinson Pearson (1856-1927), baronet of Paddockhurst, Worth, Sussex. He was created baronet in 1894, elevated to the peerage as Baron Cowdray in 1910, and as Viscount Cowdray in 1917, after serving as Lieutenant-Colonel of the Engineer and Railway Staff Corps and President of the Air Board.

This salver is one of a pair made for the 1st Duke of Cambridge and sold in the estate auction of his son, the 2nd Duke of Cambridge, in 1904. [1]

Like his brothers, George IV and the Dukes of York and Sussex, the Duke of Cambridge was an important patron of London goldsmiths in the early 19th century. At the Duke of York's auction at Christie's in 1827, the Duke of Cambridge purchased some of his brother's most important pieces of silver, including one of the Shields of Achilles designed by Flaxman for Rundell's, and a pair of monumental ewers in the mannerist style by Edward Farrell. [2] The Royal Dukes were instrumental in promoting antiquarian styles in this period; the Duke of Cambridge for example commissioned John Bridge to make reproductions of German 17th-century beakers that had been acquired by the Duke of York. [3]

The present salver is essentially an example of the rococo revival style, although in typical 19th-century fashion, it is more massive and sculptural than its George III prototypes. The mythological scenes in the border, punctuated by masks of Ceres and Bacchus, are influenced by the heavy archaeological classicism of the Regency period. The engraved armorials are in the manner of Walter Jackson, a prolific engraver whose workshop was engaged by Rundell's to engrave the armorials of numerous Royal patrons. [4]

The small maker's mark EB on this salver and its mate was thought to be that of Edward Barnard when the pair was sold in the Duke of Cambridge's sale in 1904. However, Edward Barnard was in partnership with Rebecca Emes from 1808-1829, and the marks they registered at Goldsmiths' Hall in this period include both partner's initials. The mark appears to be that of Edward Barton, who registered as a plateworker in 1822. It is logical that the retailer of this Royal commission, possibly Rundell's, subcontracted to a specialist salver maker while supplying the castings for the border. [5]

1. The mate to the present example is hallmaked 1825, and is illustrated in Michael Clayton, *Christie's Pictorial History of English and American Silver*, 1985, fig. 6, p. 287. The salvers are described as consecutive lots in Christie's Duke of Cambridge sale catalogue, 6 June 1904, lots 104 and 105. The present example was evidently sold shortly thereafter, as it now bears the engraved inscription: "Presented to Sir Weetman & Lady Pearson on their silver wedding day 1906 with the affectionate regards of his colleagues on the Board of S. Pearson & Son Ltd."
2. Catalogue of the Valuable Collection of Old English and Foreign Silver & Silver-Gilt Plate of His Royal Highness The Duke of Cambridge, Christie's, 6 June 1904, lot 107 (the Flaxman Shield of 1821), and lot 268 (the Farrell ewers of 1824). The ewers were sold at Sotheby's, New York, 16-17 December 1982, lot 541.
3. The antique German models were sold at the Duke of York's sale, Christie's, 19-22 March 1827, lot 97. Four of the "reproduction" beakers by John Bridge of 1827 were sold at Sotheby's London, 6 June 1996, lot 400, and four of 1828 were sold at Christie's, New York, 28 April 1992, lot 162. Six were included in the Duke of Cambridge's sale, Christie's, London, 6 June 1904, lot 86.
4. Charles Oman, *English Engraved Silver, 1150-1900*, London, 1978, pp. 123-126.
5. Arthur G. Grimwade, *London Goldsmiths 1697-1837*, London, rev. ed. 1990, mark 539, p. 48.

21. A WILLIAM IV SALVER

Maker's mark of Robert Garrard II
London, 1833

Diameter 25 ½ in. (64.7 cm.)
Weight 264 oz. (8228 gr.)

Engraved with the arms of De Beauvoir quartering Benyon, Powlett-Wright and others

PROVENANCE
Richard Benyon De Beauvoir (1770-1854), of Englefield House, Berkshire, who assumed the surname of Powlett-Wright in 1814 and De Beauvoir in 1822. In 1797 he married Elizabeth, daughter of Sir Francis Sykes, baronet, of Basildon Park, Berkshire.

This salver is a much more literal revival of the rococo style than the related salver in the Love Collection made for the Duke of Cambridge (cat. no. 20). However, the *horror vacui* which characterizes English taste in the second quarter of the 19th century is evident in the treatment of the flat-chased border, which in effect fills the entire field. The engraved cartouche, too, is both more exuberant and more symmetrical than typical 18th-century examples.

22. A PAIR OF VICTORIAN WINE COOLERS

After a design by Jacques-François-Joseph Saly
Probably modelled by Edward Hodges Baily
Maker's mark of John Mortimer and John Samuel Hunt
London, 1841
Stamped with retailer's signature *STORR AND MORTIMER*, pattern number *610*, and inventory numbers and weights *No.1 192* and *No.9 193.10.*

Height 14in. (35.5cm.)
Weight 382oz. (11,916gr.)

Each base with the applied cast arms of Vorontsov-Dashkov beneath a Princely Crown.

PROVENANCE
Count Ivan Iliaronovich Vorontsov-Dashkov (1790-1854) and his wife Aleksandra Kirilovna *née* Naryshkina (1817-1896)

fig. 47 Etching after J-F-J Saly, *Premier Suite de Vases antiques d'après Saly, et autres*, Paris,1746. *Courtesy Cooper-Hewitt, National Design Museum, Smithsonian Institution, Gift of the Council, 1921-6-478.*

The source of the design for this wine cooler is Jacques-François-Joseph Saly's *Suite de Vases*, a popular book of etchings dated 1746 when Saly (1717-1776) was at the French Academy in Rome (fig. 47). [1] A later engraving after Saly, the basis for the design of the present wine coolers, formed part of a design source book belonging to Storr and Mortimer. The source book contains miscellaneous designs from the mid-16th to the last quarter of the 18th centuries and is inscribed "No. 201 Storr and Mortimer, 13 New Bond St." [2]

The re-working of the Saly design into a practical source for the silversmith and the modelling of these coolers seems almost certainly to be the work of Edward Hodges Baily (1788-1857). In 1807 he moved from his home in Bristol to London where he studied under Flaxman. He appears to have helped Flaxman with his silver designs and was employed in the design studios of Rundell, Bridge and Rundell in 1815. He worked under William Theed until the latter's death in 1817 and became chief modeller following Flaxman's death in 1826. In 1833 he moved to the firm of Storr and Mortimer, the predecessor of Mortimer and Hunt (in operation from 1839-1843), later Hunt and Roskell. [3]

A third wine cooler, described perhaps more commercially as a caviar-pail, of identical design to the present pair, and with the same applied armorials, is recorded.[4] The extensive number of the original set—apparently at least ten as indicated by the inventory numbers under the bases—would suggest that these vases were originally designed as wine coolers, although their narrow proportions are unusual. It is possible that two examples from the set are referred to in 1903 by the Russian ballerina Matilda Kschessinska, when she wrote in her memoirs "the Grand Duke Wladimir Alexandrovitch...gave me wonderful presents: a pair of vases from Prince Vorontsov's collection, for instance...He had evidently grown fond of me." [5]

Count Vorontsov-Dashkov belonged to an aristocratic Russian family, some of whom are recorded living in Italy in the 1840s. [6] It is tempting to conjecture that Count Vorontsov-Dashkov ordered the wine coolers through his English cousin, Catherine, Countess of Pembroke (*née* Vorontsova).[7]

1. Bent Sorensen, "Some Drawings by Jacques Saly," *Master Drawings*, Fall 1994, vol. XXXIII no. 3, p.253.
2. "Regarding Reksten," *The Silver Society Journal,* Winter 1991, p.70.
3. Charles Oman, "A Question of Artistic Responsibility : The Firm of Rundell, Bridge & Rundell," *Apollo*, January 1966, pp.174-183.
4. Sold Anonymously, Sotheby's, London, 3 July 1969 and as part of the Hilmar Reksten Collection, Part I, Christie's, London, 22 May 1991, lot 9. Illustrated by V. Brett, *The Sotheby's Directory of Silver,* London, 1986, p.277, fig.1283.
5. H.S.H. The Princess Romanovsky-Krassinsky, *Dancing in Petersburg: The Memoirs of Kschessinska*, London, 1960, p.95.
6. F.I. Iordan, *Zapiski*, Moscow, 1918.
7. See Christie's, New York, 18 October 1994, lot 314 for a list of silver made for her stepson, the 12th Earl, in the 1830s and 1840s.

23. A VICTORIAN FIVE-PIECE TEA AND COFFEE SERVICE

Maker's mark of John Samuel Hunt
London, 1849
Stamped with retailer's signature *HUNT & ROSKELL LATE STORR MORTIMER & HUNT* and with pattern numbers *4421* through *4423*

Height of kettle 17 in. (43 cm.)
Gross weight 275 oz. (7881 gr.)

Chased with the crest and motto of Nisbet

PROVENANCE
Probably John More Nisbet (1826-1904), of Cairnhill, Lanarkshire, who married Lady Agnes Dalyrimple, daughter of the 9th Earl of Stair, on April 4, 1848
Sir Martin Wilson, Bt., Sotheby's, London, February 23, 1967, lot 85

EXHIBITED
Cooper-Hewitt Museum, New York, 1989

LITERATURE
John Culme, *Nineteenth-Century Silver*, London, 1977, p. 158.

Although designed in the tradition of the "marine rococo" styles popular in England in the George II period and again in the Regency, this tea service is by no means a mere revival of these earlier styles. This service is quintessentially mid-19th century in its absolute integration of form and ornament; the "decoration" literally dictates the shape of each object. The extremely realistic quality of the shells and coral branches, particularly in their texturing, also typifies the celebration of naturalism in the best silver designs of this period.

Hunt & Roskell's designer may have consciously drawn upon Georgian pieces in the "marine rococo" style, such as Sprimont's famous salt cellars of 1742 in the Royal Collection, which probably used castings from real crustacea and seashells. [1] However, this tea service obviously surpasses such literal realism and must have been considered a highly individual interpretation of the marine style when it was made in 1849. [2] Indeed, Hunt & Roskell exhibited pieces in the same pattern two years later at the Great Exhibition of 1851.[3] In its creativity, the service differs significantly fro Mortimer & Hunt's pair of shell-form wine-coolers of 1841, copied exactly from a French design of the 18th century (cat. no. 22). Traditionally, both the present tea service and Hunt's wine coolers have been attributed to Edward Hodges Baily, the firm's best known designer, but other artists, including Frank Howard, George Hayter, Alfred Brown, and Henry Hugh Armistead, are known to have made important models for the firm in the same period. [4] Given the variety of designers available to Hunt & Roskell, it is unlikely that the same artist designed the historically accurate wine coolers and this very innovative tea service, even though they both employ marine themes.

As the siganture on this service indicates, J.S. Hunt's firm, Hunt & Roskell, carried on the silversmithing business of Paul Storr. J.S. Hunt, Storr's nephew by

marriage, is first listed as an assistant to Storr around 1810, but was not made a partner in Storr's business until the 1820s. When Storr retired in 1838, his firm, Storr & Mortimer, was renamed Mortimer & Hunt. Upon Mortimer's retirement in 1843, the firm became Hunt & Roskell. At the time this tea service was made, Hunt & Roskell employed 35 people at their retail shop on Bond Street, and between 80 and 100 workers at their factory, including designers and modellers as well as silversmiths. The firm was a leading exhibitor in all the major international expositions of the period. [5]

1. Arthur Grimwade, *Rococo Silver*, London, 1974, pl. 37B.
2. The service originally included a toastrack formed of bulrushes similar to the kettle handle, with a double-shell base on coral feet, engraved with the same crest (Sotheby's, London, March 14, 1996, lot 47).
3. The coffeepot and sugar basin are illustrated in a review of Hunt & Roskell's exhibit, published in *The Expositor* of February 15, 1851 (reproduced in John Culme, *Nineteenth-Century Silver*, London, 1977, p. 159).
4. John Culme, *The Directory of Gold & Silversmiths, Jewellers & Allied Traders, 1838-1914*, London, 1987, vol. I, p. 246.
5. *Ibid.*, p.245, which gives a full history of the firm's partnerships and business addresses.

24. A PAIR OF VICTORIAN WINE COOLERS

Maker's mark of Jean-Valentin Morel
London, 1851

Height 8 ¾ in. (22 cm.)
Weight 245 oz. (6945 gr.)

The crest and motto are those of Bolckow

PROVENANCE
Henry William Ferdinand Bolckow, who emigrated from Mecklenburg in 1827 and was naturalized by Act of Parliament. He founded the Cleveland iron trade and became the first M.P. from Middlesbrough. He died on June 18, 1878 and was succeeded by his nephew, Carl Ferdinand Henry Bolckow, of Marton Hall, Yorkshire.
Christie's, London, June 4, 1969, lot 133

LITERATURE
John Culme, *Nineteenth-Century Silver,* London, 1977, p. 156
Michael Clayton, *Christie's Pictorial History of English and American Silver,* Oxford, 1985, fig.1, p.290 (incorrectly dated 1849)

These rare wine coolers belong to a handful of silver pieces made during the brief London career of the distinguished Parisian goldsmith, Jean-Valentin Morel (1794-1860).

Morel trained in Paris under his father, Valentin Morel (1761-1833), a lapidary, and Adrien Vachette, a goldsmith specializing in snuffboxes. By 1834, Morel had earned the position of *chef d'atelier* at the distinguished firm of Jules Fossin, *Joailliers du Roi* under Louis-Philippe. Morel left Fossin in 1842 to enter into partnership with Charles-Edmond Duponchel. [1] Morel & Duponchel's highly successful business specialized in gold and enamel-mounted hardstone objects based on Renaissance examples at the Louvre. [2]

Some time after 1844, Morel and Duponchel dissolved their partnership, resulting in a lawsuit that prohibited Morel from conducting business in the Department of the Seine. This ruling, combined with political unrest in France, led to Morel's move to London in 1848. Once there, Morel recruited and employed other French expatriate designers, including Louis-Constant Sévin (1821-1888), an important sculptor-modeller who had previously designed for Morel & Duponchel as well as for Froment-Meurice and other Parisian firms. [3] This sudden migration to London of French luxury-goods makers was undoubtedly encouraged by the Revolution of 1848, a republican uprising against the government of Louis-Philippe. Indeed, Morel, Sévin, Willms, Attarge and other artisans in Morel's circle all returned to France in 1851 and 1852, the year of the establishment of the Second Empire by Napoleon III.

Morel's brief exile in London allowed him to triumph at the Great Exhibition of 1851, where he exhibited his trademark Renaissance style hardstones, designed by Sévin and others, along with silver objects in French 18th-century taste. [4] These wine coolers, evidently inspired by Louis XIV models, seem particularly well-suited to the English preference for a rather heavy sculptural naturalism in the mid-19th century. [5]

1. Philadelphia Museum of Art, *The Second Empire: Art in France Under Napoleon III, 1978.* See Daniel Alcouffe's biography of Morel, p. 165.
2. John Culme, *Directory of Gold & Silversmiths, Jewellers & Allied Traders,* London, 1838-1914, 1987, p. 332.
3. Philadelphia Museum of Art, *op. cit.,* p. 126.
4. John Culme, *Nineteenth-Century Silver,* London, 1977, pp. 201-202.
5. Storr and Mortimer made a wine cooler of similar form in 1834, illustrated in Vanessa Brett, *The Sotheby's Directory of Silver,* London,1986, no. 1275, p. 276.

25. A VICTORIAN INKSTAND

Maker's mark of R. & S. Garrard
London, 1878
Stamped with retailer's signature *R. & S. GARRARD PANTON ST. LONDON*

Height 17 ½ in. (44.5 cm.)
Weight 300 oz. (9332 gr.)

The arms are those of Amherst, as borne by the Earls Amherst

PROVENANCE
William Pitt, 2nd Earl Amherst (1805-1886), of Montreal, Sevenoaks, Kent, who married in 1834 Gertrude, 6th daughter of the Hon. Hugh Percy, Bishop of Carlisle and brother of the 5th Duke of Northumberland. The second Earl was educated at Westminster School and Christ Church, Oxford, and was M.P. for East Grinstead, 1829-1832.

Although a functional object, this inkstand achieves the purely sculptural effect which characterizes the best of Victorian silver. Based on a baroque fountain, the design has been adapted to its use by concealing inkwells under the four hinged scallop shells in the base. The coat-of-arms and coronet of the original owner have also been incorporated into the model, directly below the Triton figure, between the dolphins' tails.

Robert Garrard II and his brother Sebastian Garrard continued the business of their father, Robert Garrard Sr., who died in 1818. This distinguished firm, which replaced Rundell's as Royal Goldsmiths in 1843, continued under the name of R. & S. Garrard & Co. until 1909, when the name changed to Garrard & Co. Ltd. Like their chief competitor in this period, Hunt & Roskell, Garrard's participated in the great international fairs of the late 19th century. [1]

1. John Culme, *The Directory of Gold & Silversmiths, Jewellers and Allied Traders, 1838-1914,* London, 1987, pp. 172-175.

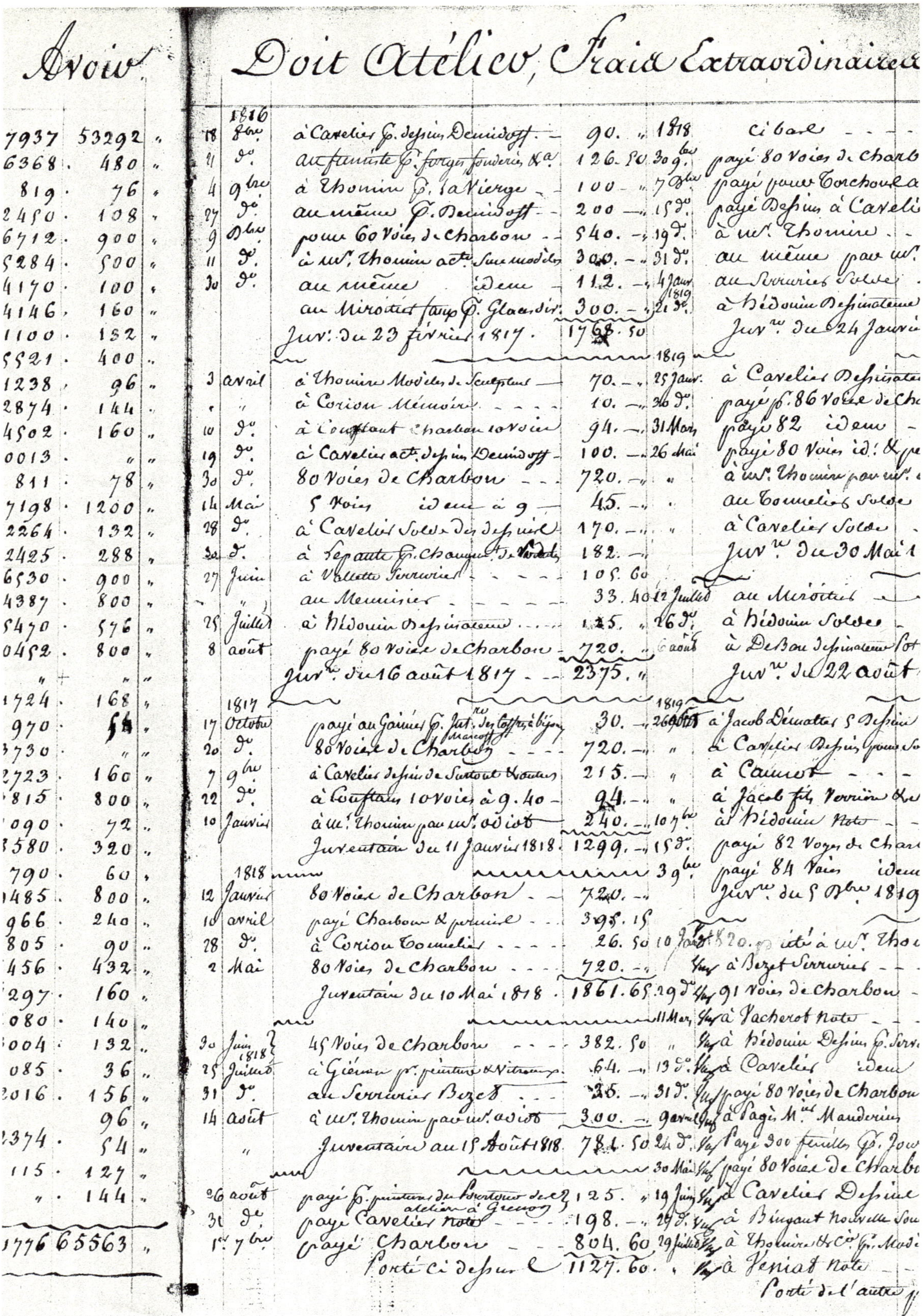

Avoir. Doit Atelier, Frais Extraordinaires

fig. 48 Odiot's workman's ledger showing payments to designers and suppliers, including Cavelier's charges for designs for the Demidoff Service. *Courtesy Olivier Gaube du Gers, Odiot.*

French
Silver-Gilt

fig. 49 The Borghese arms, from an oil-and-vinegar frame by Biennais (cat. no. 27)

THE BORGHESE SERVICE

Tradition has held that the Borghese service was a gift from Napoleon to his sister Pauline Bonaparte on the occasion of her marriage to Prince Camillo Borghese on November 6, 1803. However, the assumption that the service was a gift for this wedding is open to question, as many of the most significant pieces are signed by Biennais "*Orfèvre de Lrs. Mtés. Impériales et Royales à Paris*" which must mean that they post-date 1805 when Napoleon was styled King of Italy. In addition, many of the pieces are marked with Paris hallmarks in use between 1809 and 1819. The service, comprising roughly 500 silver-gilt objects, was primarily supplied by Martin-Guillaume Biennais, with other specialist makers contributing almost 1,000 pieces of table-silver. According to the auction catalogue of the service when it was sold in 1934, some pieces were made by Jean-Baptiste-Claude Odiot. In the 1820s various Florentine and Roman silversmiths contributed further additions made after the original designs.

The designs of Charles Percier (1764-1838) and Pierre-François-Léonard Fontaine (1762-1853) are evidently the stylistic source of the Borghese service. Percier and Fontaine probably met in 1779 when studying architecture in Paris. It was however their stay in Rome for several years after 1786 that was the basis of their future success. Their French brand of neo-classicism has been described as "a combination of severity and pomp" involving a more strictly archaeological approach than had previously been the case, drawing on a mixture of ancient styles: Greek, Imperial Roman, and, following Napoleon's campaigns of 1798-1799, Egyptian motifs as well. [1]

Winning the patronage of Empress Josephine in 1799, Percier and Fontaine became the official Imperial architects, but their enormous influence was above all the result of the publication after 1799 of numerous design books, culminating in the *Recueil de décorations intérieures*. In total the book comprised 72 plates which were issued in sets of six from 1801, and were published in full in 1812, including designs for silver and furniture, individual decorative elements, and of course views of interiors. As the authors say in their preface, "furnishings are too closely linked to interior decoration for the architect to remain indifferent to them." [2]

The work of Percier and Fontaine was perhaps best interpreted in the world of silver by the firm of Martin-Guillaume Biennais. All the pieces in the Borghese service were certainly influenced by their style, and some pieces show direct use of their designs. Biennais (1764-1843) started his career in Paris around the time of the Revolution as a *marchand-ébéniste* specialising in *nécessaires-de-voyage*, intricately fitted boxes to hold travelling services. With the outbreak of war, such services were in demand by persons of the highest rank, and the large Bonaparte family soon became his patrons. Sometime around 1800, Biennais seems to have decided to broaden his output by supplying both furniture and silver, and by 1805 had been appointed silversmith to their Imperial Majesties. Clare Le Corbeiller observes "Basically an entrepeneur employing, it is said over six hundred workmen, Biennais supplied Napoleon not only with table services but with coronation regalia, swords and sword mounts, shoe buckles, snuff boxes, tables, cabinets and, of course, *nécessaires*. In view of his background and this heterogeneous activity, the consistent refinement and elegance of his work in silver is remarkable." [3]

Pauline Bonaparte was born in 1780 in Ajaccio, Corsica, the second of Napoleon's sisters and considered to be the most beautiful. In 1797 she married one of her brother's staff officers, General C-V-E Leclerc, and went with him to Santo Domingo. Following his early death from yellow fever, she returned to Paris, met and married Prince Borghese, and moved to Rome. In 1804, Borghese received the title of a French Prince, and in the following years accompanied the Emperor in the Austrian and Prussian campaigns. Nonetheless, his marriage with Pauline Borghese was an unhappy one and they separated fairly quickly. Following the Treaty of Tilsit he was made Governor of Piedmont. He was paid the huge sum of 1 million francs which, added to his own fortune, allowed him to live in the grandest style. In the meantime his wife spent most of her time in Paris and with the fall of Napoleon in 1814 she tried to gain permission to join him in exile in Saint Helena. When this was denied she returned to Rome and took up residence in the Borghese Palace. She did however join her husband in Florence shortly before her death in 1825.

It has been suggested that Pauline Borghese was responsible for many of the later additions to the service, but it is at least as likely that Prince Borghese himself ordered these pieces. [4] It is certainly possible that the service was split between the Roman and Florentine residences and that both of them added to it. The service remained at the Borghese Palace in Rome until it was sold in the auction of the Palace contents in 1892. The service was listed in its entirety in the auction catalogue entitled *Catalogue des objets d'art et d'ameublement. Le grand appartement au premier étage du palais du Prince Borghese à Rome*, and was offered as a single lot. The service appears to have subsequently changed hands at least three times before becoming part of the collection of the American Edith Rockefeller McCormick, who exhibited the entire service from 1924-1932 at the Chicago Art Institute. On her death in 1934, the service was sold by the American Art Association/Anderson Galleries in New York where it was split into nearly 150 lots. Pieces from the Borghese service are now widely scattered, with objects in many private collections and museums, including the Metropolitan Museum of Art, New York. [5]

1. Charles Percier and Pierre-François-Léonard Fontaine, *Recueil de décorations intérieures*, Dover Reprint, New York, 1991, p.iii.
2. *Ibid*, p.xi.
3. Clare Le Corbeiller, "An Introduction to Napoleonic Silver," in the exhibition catalogue, *The Arts Under Napoleon*, The Metropolitan Museum of Art, New York, 1978.
4. See Sotheby's, Geneva, 14 November, 1988, lot 94.
5. Faith Dennis, *Three Centuries of French Domestic Silver*, New York, 1960, vol.I, cat. nos. 63-65 and 265.

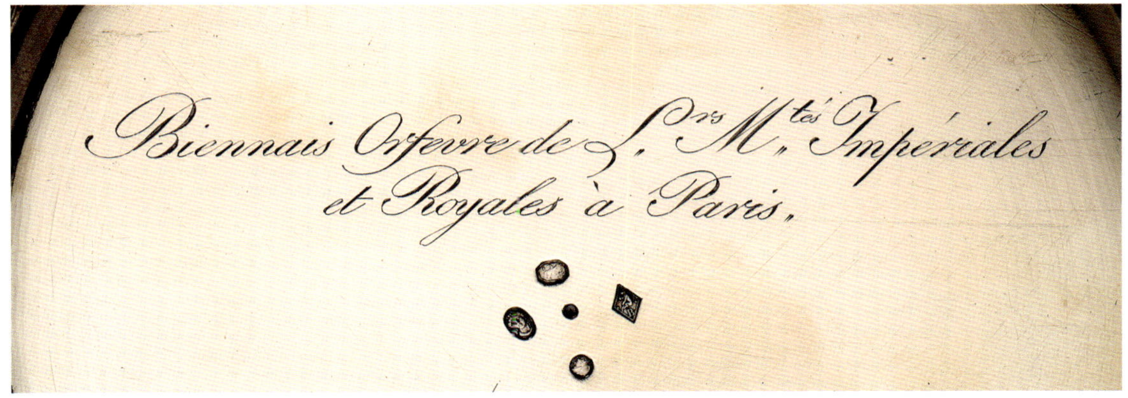

fig. 50 Engraved inscription and hallmarks from the wine coolers by Biennais from the Borghese Service (cat. no. 26)

26. A PAIR OF WINE COOLERS FROM THE BORGHESE SERVICE

Maker's mark of Martin-Guillaume Biennais
Paris, 1809-1819
Silver-plated copper liners unmarked
The bases engraved *Biennais Orfèvre de lrs. mtés. Impériales et Royales à Paris.*

Height 8 ⅞in. (22.5 cm.)
Weight 151oz. (4,705gr.)

Applied with the arms of Borghese as borne by Prince Camillo Borghese

PROVENANCE
Prince Camillo Borghese, who married Pauline Bonaparte, sister of the Emperor Napoleon, on 6 November 1803
The Borghese Palace sale, Giacomini and Capobianchi, Rome, 28 March-9 April 1892, part of lot 847
Don Antonio Licata
Prince Baucina
Ercole Canessa
Mrs. Edith Rockefeller McCormick, American Art Association/Anderson Galleries Inc., New York, 5 January 1934, either lot 699 or 700

EXHIBITED
The Art Institute of Chicago, June 1924-November 1932, as part of the entire service
The Metropolitan Museum of Art, New York, "The Arts Under Napoleon," 6 April- 30 July 1978, cat. no.150, fig.30.

Originally two of four, these fine wine coolers typify Biennais's elegant and restrained work at its best. Although no drawing for them is included among Percier's designs published by Hessling in 1911, the basic form and elements of the decoration all point to Percier as the designer. Biennais re-used this design for a wine-cooler made for Grand Duke Nicholas Pavlovitch, later Emperor Nicholas I. [1]

1. Sold at Sotheby's, Geneva, 14 November 1988, lot 101.

27. TWO FRENCH OIL-AND-VINEGAR FRAMES FROM THE BORGHESE SERVICE

Based on designs by Charles Percier
Maker's mark of Martin-Guillaume Biennais
Paris, one 1798-1809, the other 1809-1819

a) Height 10 ¾in. (27.3 cm.)
b) Height 10 ⅜ in. (26.7 cm.)
Weight 114oz. (3,568 gr.)

Applied with the arms of Borghese as borne by Prince Camillo Borghese

PROVENANCE
Prince Camillo Borghese, who married Pauline Bonaparte, the sister of the Emperor Napoleon, on 6 November 1803
The Borghese Palace sale, Giacomini and Capobianchi, Rome, 28 March-9 April 1892, part of lot 847
Don Antonio Licata
Prince Baucina
Ercole Canessa
Mrs. Edith Rockefeller McCormick, American Art Association/Anderson Galleries Inc., New York, 5 January 1934, lot 669 and 670

EXHIBITED
The Art Institute of Chicago, June 1924-November 1932 as part of the entire service
The Metropolitan Museum of Art, New York, "The Arts Under Napoleon," 6 April -30 July 1978, cat. no. 153

The figure of Victory, which forms the handles on these oil and vinegar frames, closely follows two designs by Percier (figs. 51 and 52). Biennais also adapted this model for the double salt cellars in the Borghese service.

It has been suggested that the matching frame in the Love Collection which is slightly smaller than the example illustrated here, is a later casting by Biennais. [1] However, the difference in height within the present pair is probably due to an old break above the feet, causing the figure to be reset at an angle. [2]

1. Exhibition Catalogue, *The Arts Under Napoleon,* The Metropolitan Museum of Art, New York, 1978, cat no. 153.
2. The marks on the smaller example do not appear to be cast, except on one wreath which is replaced.

fig. 51 Design for an-oil-and vinegar frame by Charles Percier, from Armand Guérinet, ed., *Recueil de dessins d'orfèvrerie du Premier Empire, par Biennais, orfèvre de Napoléon Ier et de la Couronne*, Paris, 1911, pl. 6. *Courtesy New York Public Library.*

fig. 52 Design for an-oil-and vinegar frame by Charles Percier, from Armand Guérinet, ed., *Recueil de dessins d'orfèvrerie du Premier Empire, par Biennais, orfèvre de Napoléon Ier et de la Couronne*, Paris, 1911, pl. 42. *Courtesy New York Public Library.*

28. A PAIR OF FRENCH DISHES, COVERS AND COPPER-GILT STANDS FROM THE BORGHESE SERVICE

Based on a design by Charles Percier
Maker's mark of Martin-Guillaume Biennais
Paris, 1809-1819
Stands unmarked
The interior of the covers engraved *Biennais Orfre. de lrs. mtés. Impériales et Royales à Paris*

Diameter of dishes 11 ¾in. (30 cm.)
Weight of covers and dishes 308 oz. (9,601 gr.)

Engraved with the arms of Borghese as borne by Prince Camillo Borghese

PROVENANCE
Prince Camillo Borghese who married Pauline Bonaparte, the sister of the Emperor Napoleon, on 6 November 1803
The Borghese Palace sale, Giacomini and Capobianchi, Rome, 28 March-9 April 1892, part of lot 847
Don Antonio Licata
Prince Baucina
Ercole Canessa
Mrs. Edith Rockefeller McCormick, American Art Association/Anderson Galleries Inc., New York, 5 January 1934, the stands and covers two of five pairs of this size sold as lots 732-736; the dishes are two of five pairs sold as lots 717-721

EXHIBITED
The Art Institute of Chicago, June 1924-November 1932, as part of the entire service

The decoration of the dish covers or cloches are, with the exception of the finials, based on a design by Percier (fig. 53).[1] The bud finial has an unusual feature in that by rotating it, the calyx below turns to reveal piercing, both as a decorative element and to release steam.

1. The design is reproduced in two publications: E. Hessling, ed., *Documents de style Empire. Dessins d'orfèvrerie de Percier conservés à la Bibliothèque de L'Union Centrale des arts décoratifs de Paris,* Paris, 1911, pl. 20, and Armand Guérinet, ed., *Recueil de dessin d'orfèvrerie du Premier Empire par Biennais orfèvre de Napoléon Ier et de la Couronne,* 1911, vol. XXII, pl. 35.

fig. 53 Design for a dish cover by Charles Percier, from E. Hessling, ed., *Documents de Style Empire. Dessins d'orfèvrerie de Percier...,* Paris, 1911, pl. 20. *Courtesy New York Public Library.*

29. THREE PAIRS OF COASTERS FROM THE BORGHESE SERVICE

a) One pair, maker's mark of Martin-Guillaume Biennais
   Paris, 1798-1809
b) Second pair, maker's mark of the workshop of the Brothers Scheggi, Florence, circa 1825
c) Third pair, Rome, circa 1820, maker's mark omitted

a) Diameter 4 ⅞ in. (12.3 cm.)
b) Diameter 3 ⅞ in. (12.3 cm.)
c) Diameter 3 ⅞ in. (9.8 cm.)
a) Weight 17 oz. (510 gr.)
b) Weight 20 oz. (576 gr,)
c) Weight 13 oz. (372 gr.)

Each engraved with the arms of Borghese as borne by Prince Camillo Borghese

PROVENANCE
Prince Camillo Borghese, who married Pauline Bonaparte, the sister of the Emperor Napoleon, on 6 November 1803
The Borghese Palace sale, Giacomini and Capobianchi, Rome, 28 March-9 April 1892, part of lot 847
Don Antonio Licata
Prince Baucina
Ercole Canessa
Mrs. Edith Rockefeller McCormick, American Art Association/Anderson Galleries Inc., New York, 5 January 1934 a) and b) four of 32 sold as sets of eight, lots 671 and 676-678; c) two of 32 sold as sets of eight, lots 672-675

EXHIBITED
The Art Institute of Chicago, June 1924-November 1932 as part of the entire service

It seems probable that the thirty-two larger coasters originally in the Borghese service held wine bottles and the same number of smaller coasters, including the present Italian examples, were for wine glasses.

Prince Borghese spent much of his time in Florence following the defeat of Napoleon, and turned to silversmiths there to enlarge his French service. The difference in quality between the Biennais originals and the Italian copies is striking—neither the piercing nor the engraving on the later examples is as fine. The identification of the Florentine makers is complicated by the fact that at least four members of the Scheggi family, the brothers Luigi and Vincenzo and the latter's sons Angelo and Ferdinando, all used the same maker's mark around 1825.

The Scheggi brothers published in 1797-1798 a number of silver models in the *Magazzino di Mobilia.* In 1816, Grand Duke Ferdinand III of Tuscany commissioned the Scheggis, together with silversmiths Gaetano Guadagni and Andrea Marchesini, to add to the Duke's own French table service, also by Biennais. [1]

Unfortunately the Roman coasters are not struck with a maker's mark but only the post-1815 town mark and the standard mark for silver which most closely approximates the purity of French silver. In all probability the coasters were made by Pietro Paolo Spagna (w. 1817-1861), who supplied additional silver to the Borghese service. It is likely that the Roman coasters were ordered by the Princess Borghese, who lived in Rome from 1814 to 1828. [2]

1. See Dora Liscia Bemporad, *et al.*, *Argenti Fiorentini*, Florence, 1993, pp. 434-5 for details on the Scheggi family.
2. A coffeepot from the Borghese service by Spagna was sold at Sotheby's, Geneva, 14 November 1988, lot 94.

29c

29b

29a

30. A PAIR OF FRENCH MUSTARD POTS FROM THE BORGHESE SERVICE

Based on a design by Charles Percier
Maker's mark of Martin-Guillaume Biennais
Paris, 1809-1819

Height 5 in. (12 cm.)
Weight 23 oz. (743 gr.)

Engraved with the arms of Borghese as borne by Prince Camillo Borghese

PROVENANCE
Prince Camillo Borghese, who married Pauline Bonaparte, sister of the Emperor Napoleon, on 6 November 1803
The Borghese Palace sale, Giacomini and Capobianchi, Rome, 28 March-9 April 1892, part of lot 847
Don Antonio Licata
Prince Baucina
Ercole Canessa
Mrs. Edith Rockefeller McCormick, American Art Association/Anderson Galleries Inc., New York, 5 January 1934, lot 656

EXHIBITED
The Art Institute of Chicago, June 1924-November 1932 as part of the entire service.
The Metropolitan Museum of Art, New York, "The Arts Under Napoleon," 6 April- 30 July 1978, cat. no.152, fig. 29

Charles Percier's designs for similar mustard pots all show more shallow glass liners which reveal the coats-of-arms in the center of the bases (fig. 54). [1] The glass liners in the present mustard pots which obscure the coats-of-arms are, then, almost certainly replacements. Elements from two designs by Percier appear to be the basis for the mustard-pots in the Borghese service. In one, the swan supports, tight scroll handle and shape of the cover are visible, while the other provides the pattern for the border decoration. The triangular base with cut corners and laurel leaf banding is presumably taken from a third unrecorded design. [2]

1. Exhibition Catalogue, *The Arts Under Napoleon,* The Metropolitan Museum of Art, New York, 1978, cat. no. 152.
2. These designs are reproduced in two publications: E. Hessling, ed., *Documents du style Empire. Dessins d'orfèvrerie de Percier conservés à la bibliothèque de L'Union Centrale des arts décoratifs de Paris,* Paris, 1911, pl.9, and Armand Guérinet, ed., *Recueil de dessin d'orfèvrerie du Premier Empire par Biennais, orfèvre de Napoleon Ier et de la Couronne,* 1911, vol.XXII.

fig. 54 Design for a mustard pot by Charles Percier from E. Hessling, ed., *Documents de style Empire. Dessins d'orfèvrerie de Percier...*, Paris, 1911, pl. 9. *Courtesy New York Public Library*.

31. A SET OF FOUR FRENCH *POTS-A-CREME* FROM THE BORGHESE SERVICE

Maker's mark of Martin-Guillaume Biennais
Paris, 1809-1819

Overall length 5 ¼in. (13.4cm.)
Diameter of bowls 2 ¾in. (7cm.)
Weight with handles 17oz. (543gr.)

Engraved with the arms of Borghese as borne by Prince Camillo Borghese

PROVENANCE
Prince Camillo Borghese, who married Pauline Bonaparte, the sister of the Emperor Napoleon on 6 November 1803
The Borghese Palace sale, Giacomini and Capobianchi, Rome, 28 March-9 April 1892, part of lot 847
Don Antonio Licata
Prince Baucina
Ercole Canessa
Mrs. Edith Rockefeller McCormick, American Art Association/Anderson Galleries Inc., New York, 5 January 1934

EXHIBITED
The Art Institute of Chicago, June 1924-November 1932 as part of the entire service

The original function of these pots, four of seven in the Love Collection, has been much debated. Similar covered cups with heat resistant handles are found in pre-Revolutionary France. [1] It has been suggested in the past that *pots-à-crème* were *pöelons de table,* individual casseroles for portions of truffles, eggs or *ortollans* to be used as condiments for the main course. [2] However, 18th-century menus and recipes suggest that pots of this type were used not for liquid cream or for condiments but rather for individual cooked and flavored cream-dishes which were served as *entremets,* or side dishes. One mid-18th century cookbook lists 32 different recipes for these cream-dishes, mostly cooked in a hot water tub known as a *bain-marie.* [3] That these cream-dishes continued to be made into the 19th century is confirmed by an inventory of 1816 for a large Napoleonic dinner-service which included 18 *pots-à-crème.* [4]

It seems that a related type of small cauldron-shaped pot *(pot-à-bouchée)* with three feet, a cover and a swing handle, was also intended for cooked cream-dishes. [5] This type of pot was often made in the workshop of Jean-François Carron but was also much imitated in the 19th and early part of this century.

1. For an 18th century example by Pierre François Goguely, Paris, 1778 in the Metropolitan Museum of Art, New York, see Faith Dennis, *Three Centuries of French Domestic Silver,* New York, 1960, vol.I, p.131, cat. no.172.
2. Dennis, *op.cit.,* cat. no.172, and *Inventaire général des monuments et des richesses artistiques de la France, objets civils domestiques. Vocabulaire typologique,* Paris, 1984, p.128.
3. *Dictionnaire des alimens, vins et liqueurs . . .,* by M.C.D. Chef de Cuisine de M. Le Prince ****, Paris, 1750, vol.I, pp. 434-442.
4. According to P. Villard, 18 *pots-à-crème* are listed in the service made for Napoleon as King of Italy, which later became the service at the Court of Austria. See "*Service de Napoleon Ier, Roi d'Italie ou Le Grand Cour Imperiale de Vienne,*" in the exhibition catalogue, *Versailles et les Tables Royales en Europe,* XVIIème-XIXème siècles, Versailles, November 1993-February 1994, cat. nos. 314-327.
5. *Objets civiles domestiques, op.cit.,* p.128, fig.628. A pair of these pots by Carron, Paris, 1781, now in the Musée des arts Décoratifs, is illustrated in Gérard Mabille, *Orfèvrerie française des XVIe XVIIe XVIIIe siècles,* Paris, 1984, p.44, fig.54.

32. A PAIR OF FRENCH GRAVY SPOONS FROM THE BORGHESE SERVICE

Maker's mark of Pierre-Benoît Lorillon
Paris, 1809-1819

Length 11 ¾in. (29.8 cm.)
Weight 11 oz. (354 gr.)

Engraved with the arms of Borghese as borne by Prince Camillo Borghese

PROVENANCE
Prince Camillo Borghese, who married Pauline Bonaparte, sister of the Emperor Napoleon, on 6 November 1803
The Borghese Palace sale, Giacomini and Capobianchi, Rome, 28 March-9 April 1892, part of lot 847
Don Antonio Licata
Prince Baucina
Ercole Canessa
Mrs. Edith Rockefeller McCormick, American Art Association/Anderson Galleries Inc., New York, 5 January 1934, two of twelve sold in sets of six, lots 642 and 643

EXHIBITED
The Art Institute of Chicago, June 1924-November 1932 as part of the entire service

Just as the table-silver in the Demidoff service was supplied to Odiot by the specialist maker François-Dominique Naudin, so Biennais commissioned Lorillon and others to supply the bulk of the table-silver in the Borghese service. This immense commission of almost a thousand pieces of table-silver required supplementary pieces by Naudin, Michel Kinon and Aimée-Catherine Cléri. Biennais's and even Odiot's marks are also found on pieces of table-silver from the Borghese service.

33. A FRENCH SWEETMEAT DISH ON STAND

Maker's mark of Jean-Baptiste-Claude Odiot
Paris, 1809-1819

Overall length 5 ¾ in. (14.5 cm.)
Weight 15 oz. (464 gr.)

A number of small detachable dishes on stands with butterfly handles by Odiot are recorded. The best known are the pair in the English Royal Collection which are thought to have originally been intended for use as small oil lamps. [1] Each has a stand formed as a satyr supporting a bowl formed as a woman's breast, said to have been modelled after Napoleon's sister, Pauline Borghese, who was affectionately known as "the butterfly."

Although this origin for the bowls has been questioned, it is interesting to recall the Sèvres porcelain bowls of the 1780s and their Capo di Monte copies, which are thought to have been modelled on the breast of Marie-Antoinette.

The Prince Regent, like so many other Englishmen including the Duke of Wellington himself, patronized Odiot immediately after the Napoleonic Wars. On 30 November 1815, he purchased a bowl with butterfly handle on a satyr stand described in Odiot's accounts as *"formant sein de Vénus."* [2] Evidently the Prince Regent bought a second unmounted breast-form bowl at the same time and had Rundell's add a butterfly handle and stand which were marked by Paul Storr in 1816. [3] These bowls and another in the collection of Maison Odiot are thought to be based on a design for Odiot by Prud'hon. [4] The butterfly handles continued to be used on less exotic bowls, as on the present example.

1. J-M. Pinçon and O. Gaube du Gers, *Odiot l'orfèvre,* Paris 1990, pp.110-111 and figs. 172-175.
2. *Carlton House: The Past Glories of George IV's Palace,* London, 1991, cat. no. 98, p. 135.
3. *Ibid.,* p. 135.
4. *Les grands orfèvres de Louis XII à Charles X,* preface by J. Helft, Paris, 1965, p.302 and fig.1.

34. A PAIR OF FRENCH FIVE-LIGHT CANDELABRA

Maker's mark of Martin-Guillaume Biennais
Paris, 1809-1819
The bases engraved *Biennais Orfèvre à Paris*

Height 20 in. (52 cm.)
Weight 226 oz. (7,041 gr.)

Many of Biennais's candelabra incorporate the club-shaped stems and horn-shaped branches found on the Love examples. This basic form is derived from designs of Percier and Fontaine for a much grander and more richly decorated example (fig. 55). [1] A pair of silver-gilt candelabra from the Borghese service, another pair by Biennais of 1798-1809, and the present examples all have a central light that differs from the outer lights. The branches of the two related pairs differ from those on the present example in that the foliate scrolls centering paterae are set above the branches rather than below. [2]

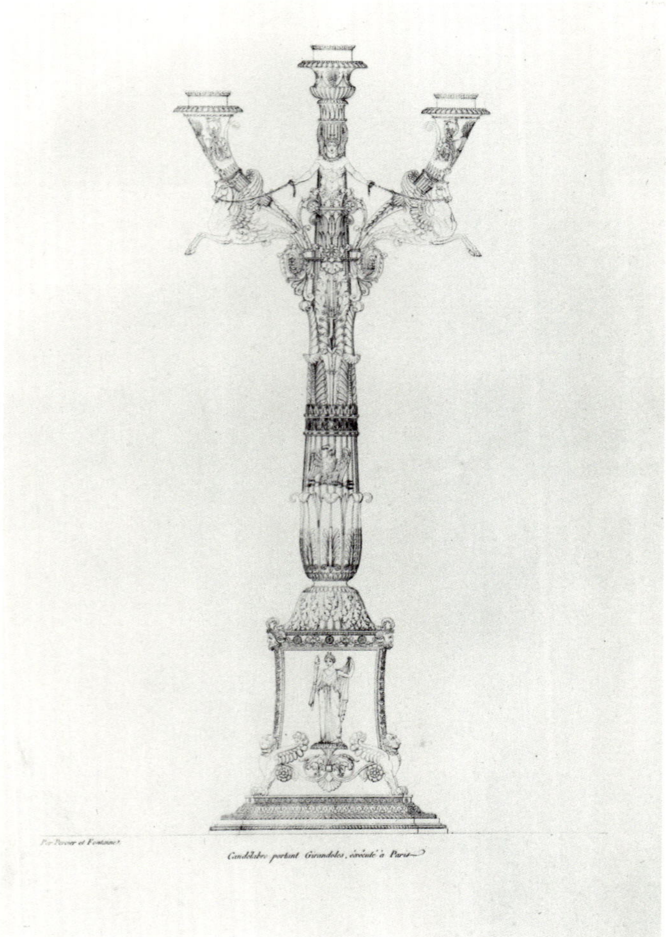

Many of the same features appear in another, still later, pair of silver candelabra with the maker's mark of Jean-Charles Cahier, 1819-1838, and the applied monogram of Grand Duke Mikhail Pavlovitch, the fourth son of the Russian Emperor Paul I. [3] Cahier's workshop and that of Biennais jointly produced the massive Pavlovitch service; in some cases their marks appear on different parts of the same piece. In 1819, Biennais retired and sold his business to Cahier, including the archives and designs. It may well be that the large expenditure involved in purchasing Biennais's business in 1821 contributed to Cahier's bankruptcy in 1828.

fig. 55 Design for "*Candélabre portant girandoles*," from Percier and Fontaine's *Recueil de décorations intérieures*, Paris, 1812.

1. Charles Percier and Pierre Fontaine, *Recueil de décorations intérieures*, Paris, 1812, pl. 59.
2. The Borghese pair, now in the Metropolitan Museum of Art, is illustrated in Faith Dennis, *Three Centuries of French Domestic Silver*, New York, 1960, vol. 1, fig. 65, p.77. The pair of 1798-1809 sold at Christie's, Geneva, 19 November 1996, lot 51.
3. Sold at Christie's, Geneva, 19 November 1996, lot 37.

35. A FRENCH CUP AND SAUCER

Based on a drawing by Antoine-Léonard Dupasquier
Maker's mark of Jean-Baptiste-Claude Odiot
Paris, circa 1806

Overall height 4 ¼in. (11cm.)
Weight 15 oz. (496 gr.)

This elegant cup and saucer closely follows a design by the sculptor Antoine-Léonard Dupasquier (c.1748-1832) (figs. 56 and 57). [1] The working drawing shows two alternative bands of foliage around the neck, one for the anthemion and the other for vine leaves and grapevines. The engraver of this cup has followed the latter although varied the placing of the leaves and grapes slightly, while the stiff foliage engraved around the lower part of the body and the cast scroll and foliage handle are identical to the design.

The engraved initial *N* is apparently not contemporary with the piece. A more elaborate initial *N* and engraved coat-of-arms are found on a teapot, tea caddy, and cup, all by Biennais and known to have been looted from Napoleon's carriage by Prussian troops following his defeat at Waterloo in 1815. [2] A knife and fork also by Biennais were left behind during the Emperor's retreat after the Battle of Leipzig in 1813. [3] It is possible however that pieces of silver given by Napoleon as official gifts were later engraved by the recipients, and that this cup is an example of such commemorative engraving.

1. Reproduced in J-M Pinçon and O. Gaube du Gers, *Odiot l'orfèvre*, Paris 1990, p.171, fig. 268
2. Christie's Geneva, 19 November 1996, lot 49
3. Christie's New York, 14 March 1984, lot 31

fig. 56 Design for a cup by A-L Dupasquier for Odiot, circa 1806. *Courtesy Olivier Gaube du Gers, Odiot.*

fig. 57 Design for a cup by A-L Dupasquier for Odiot, circa 1806. *Courtesy Olivier Gaube du Gers, Odiot.*

36. A FRENCH TEA CADDY

Maker's mark of Jean-Baptiste-Claude Odiot
Paris, 1809-1819

Height 6 in. (15.2 cm.)
Weight 24 oz. (748 gr.)

EXHIBITED
The Metropolitan Museum of Art, New York, "The Arts Under Napoleon," 6 April-30 July 1978, cat. no. 166

Although it has been suggested that this elegant architectural caddy was designed as part of a centerpiece, its rectangular shape with flat sliding cover is typical of tea caddies. [1] Odiot made a number of caddies of this form. The applied scene on the side of the present example depicting the infant Bacchus riding a panther and holding a thyrsus and tazza is found on another Odiot caddy, part of a magnificent travelling service with the arms of Napoleon. [2] Odiot used the same scene on yet another silver-gilt tea caddy and also on a teapot, of 1819-1838 and 1826-1838 respectively, both now in the Victoria and Albert Museum, London. [3] The museum acquired its tea caddy and teapot along with a covered sugar bowl by Odiot of 1809-1819, which is supported by three kneeling bacchanalian infants identical to the finial on the present caddy. [4] The continued application of the same cast decorative elements on diverse objects is characteristic of Odiot's work.

1. Exhibition catalogue, *The Arts Under Napoleon,* Metropolitan Museum of Art, New York, 1978, cat. no.166.
2. J-M Pinçon and O. Gaube du Gers, *Odiot l'orfèvre,* Paris, 1900, p.77, fig.107.
3. R.W. Lightbown, *French Silver,* London, 1978, pp.110-111, cat. no. 111, and pp.111- 112, cat. no. 112.
4. *Ibid*., pp.110-111, cat. no. 110.

37. A PAIR OF FRENCH DOUBLE SALT-CELLARS

Based on drawings by Auguste Moreau and Adrien-Louise-Marie Cavelier
Maker's mark of Jean-Baptiste-Claude Odiot
Paris, 1798-1809

Height 12 ½in. (31.8cm.)
Weight 119oz. (3,707gr.)

These beautiful salt cellars seem to epitomise Odiot's work at its best and indeed have been described as "*un des grands classiques de l'orfèvre.*" [1] The model was reused by Jean-Baptiste-Claude Odiot's son, Charles-Nicolas, between 1826 and 1838 for a set of six examples in the collection of the King of Sweden. In addition to the working drawing and finished design for the present salt cellars, Odiot's archives contain a design for a mustard or jam pot with an identical standing figure (figs. 58-60).

1. J-M. Pinçon and O. Gaube du Gers, *Odiot l'orfèvre*, Paris, 1990, p.113, and figs. 178 and 179.

fig. 58 Design for a double salt cellar, by A-L-M Cavelier for Odiot, circa 1806. *Courtesy Olivier Gaube du Gers, Odiot.*

fig. 59 Design for a double salt cellar, by Auguste Garneray for Odiot, circa 1809. *Courtesy Olivier Gaube du Gers, Odiot.*

fig. 60 Design for a mustard or jam pot, by A-L-M Cavelier for Odiot, circa 1809. *Courtesy Olivier Gaube du Gers, Odiot.*

38. A FRENCH *NECESSAIRE-DE-VOYAGE*

Maker's mark of Martin-Guillaume Biennais
Paris, 1809-1819
the mahogany case signed *Biennais Orfèvre de L.L.M.M. Imples. et Royales*

The upper part of the brass-bound mahogany case containing:

a basin, 9 in. (23 cm.) long, signed *Biennais*
two covered pots, 2 ¼in. (5.8 cm.) high, signed *Biennais*
a covered shaving pot with detachable handle, 2 ¼ in. (5.8 cm.) high, signed *Biennais*
a combined inkwell and sander, 2 ¼ in. (5.8 cm.) high, signed *Biennais*
a double box, 2 ¼ in. (5.8 cm.) high
a box containing seal with detachable handle, 1 ¾ in. (4.5 cm.) high
six various silver-gilt mounted glass scent-bottles, 2 ⅛ in. (5.5 cm.) high
an easel mirror with alternate suspension ring, 8 in. (21.5 cm.) high

The lower part with fifteen various instruments including:
a silver-gilt mounted tooth-brush
a gold-mounted mother-of-pearl handled pen-knife
a razor strop
two metal boot-jacks

Overall length of case 10 in. (25.5cm.)
Weighable silver 17 oz. (549 gr.)

The case is engraved with an Imperial eagle beneath a crown and the inscription *Donné par S.A.I. Le Prince Louis Napoléon à M. Armand Laity, Château de Ham le 5 août 1843*

PROVENANCE
Armand Laity (b.1806), a leading Bonapartist under Napoleon III

This *nécessaire* is of considerable historical importance as well as being a fine, if rather small, example of the travelling cases with which Biennais first established his name.

Armand Laity, the recipient of this gift from Prince Louis Napoleon, later Napoleon III, conspired with the Prince in the attempted capture of Strasbourg in 1836. Two years later, Laity published an account of the affair in a pamphlet entitled *Relation historique des événements du 30 octobre 1836. Le Prince Napoléon à Strasbourg*. Although acquitted of treason for his activities at Strasbourg, he was tried and convicted for publishing the pamphlet, one of the first Bonapartist tracts. In addition to paying a 10,000 franc fine, he was sentenced to five years imprisonment which made him a hero and a martyr to the re-emerging Bonapartist cause. An account of his trial was published in 1838 entitled *Procès de Armand Laity...accusé devant la Cour des Paris du crime d'attentat contre la sureté de l'état comme l'auteur de l'écrit intitulé: Relation historique...Recueilli par B. Saint-Edmé.*

A second attempted insurrection at Boulogne resulted in the capture of Prince Louis Napoleon. He was imprisoned in the Château (or Citadel) de Ham and must have arranged for the gift of this *nécessaire* to Laity while there. Finally, he escaped on May 25,1846, arriving in London two days later. [1] Prince Louis Napoleon returned to France to become President in 1848 and Emperor from 1852-1870. In this period, Laity naturally became a leading member of the Court.

Biennais specialized in the production of *nécessaires-de-voyage* from the outset of his career. By 1789 when he was 25, he had set up his shop at the "*Singe Violet*" in the rue Saint-Honoré in Paris as a *tabletier* or maker and seller of small luxury objects such as table games, boxes and cane handles of various materials such as ivory, tortoise-shell, and exotic woods. [2] The mid-19th century French silversmith François-Desiré Froment-Meurice recalled that Biennais was a "complete stranger to *orfèvrerie*: not even the pieces of silver in the *nécessaires* he sold were made on the premises." [3] Again according to

Froment-Meurice, Biennais allowed several of the young officers in the Egyptian and Italian campaigns, including possibly Napoleon himself, to take their *nécessaires* on credit. He was amply rewarded when they returned victorious, paid him in full, and eventually became some of his leading patrons.

1. See F.T. Biffault, *The Prisoner of Ham: Authentic Details of the Captivity and Escape of Prince Louis Napoleon*, London, 1846.
2. Hugh Honour, *Goldsmiths and Silversmiths*, New York, 1971, p.233.
3. As quoted by Honour, *op.cit.*, p.234.

39. A PAIR OF FRENCH JEWEL CASKETS

Based on a drawing by Auguste Garneray after Adrien-Louise-Marie Cavelier, circa 1810
Maker's mark of Jean-Baptiste-Claude Odiot
Paris, 1819-1838

Length 10 ⅞ in. (27.6 cm.)
Weight 320 oz. (9,973 gr.)

These beautifully designed and executed caskets closely follow the drawing by Garneray after Cavelier's design for a jewel casket for the Empress Marie-Louise, circa 1810 (figs. 63 and 65). [1] While the drawing for the Imperial casket indicates that the panels were to be mother-of-pearl applied with silver decoration, the design of the applied ornament is almost identical to that on the Love caskets. This ornament, comprised of paired grotesques with tails of scrolling acanthus, is based on antique Roman motifs (fig. 61).

Two further designs in the collection of Odiot for another casket have the same somewhat erotic finials of winged putti as found on the present caskets (figs. 62 and 64). [2] Indeed, the iconography of the two putti—one pouring water next to a growing sapling and the other tasting ripened fruit—may be seen as male and female, together symbolizing conjugal love. Such themes are typical of marriage presents, and the heart-shaped reserve with initial L reiterates the subject of love. [3] A similar casket is known to have been given by the Russian Emperor Alexander I to Princess Gargarine. [4]

1. The design for the Empress Marie-Louise's casket is reproduced in J-M Pinçon and O. Gaube du Gers, *Odiot l'orfèvre,* Paris, 1990, p.138
2. The design for this casket is reproduced in *Les grands orfèvres de Louis XIII à Charles X,* preface by Jacques Helft, Paris, 1965, p.266.
3. At first sight, the applied heart enclosing the script initial L, which replaces an escutcheon on the design for the Marie-Louise casket, might appear to be a later 19th century addition, but close examination shows that it is struck with the same Paris guarantee mark of 1819-1838 as the other applied details.
4. J-M Pinçon and O. Gaube du Gers, *op.cit,* p.138. Odiot's account which would have recorded the original owner of the caskets in the Love Collection is now missing.

fig. 61 Paired grotesques from Carletti's *Le antiche camere delle Terme di Tito e le loro pitture,* Rome, 1776, a work widely circulated in Europe and particularly popular in France.

cat. no. 39 detail

fig. 62 Design for a jewel casket for Odiot, circa 1810. *Courtesy Olivier Gaube du Gers, Odiot.*

fig. 63 Design for a jewel casket for Empress Marie-Louise, circa 1810. *Courtesy Olivier Gaube du Gers, Odiot.*

cat. no. 39 detail

fig. 64 Design for a jewel casket for Odiot, circa 1810. *Courtesy Olivier Gaube du Gers, Odiot.*

fig. 65 Design for a jewel casket for Empress Marie-Louise, by A.Garneray after A-L-M Cavelier for Odiot, circa 1810. *Courtesy Olivier Gaube du Gers, Odiot.*

40. A FRENCH PRESENTATION CUP

Based on a drawing by Prud'hon and Cavelier after a design by Henri Auguste
Maker's mark of Jean-Baptiste-Claude Odiot
Paris, circa 1819

Overall height 19 ¾ in. (50.2 cm.)
Weight 230 oz. (6,520 gr.)

The plinth engraved:

A SIR DAVID DUNDAS BARONNET
LES PRINCESSES
DE NOAILLES DE POIX,
D'ALSACE-CHIMAY-D'HENIN,
DE TALLEYRAND-PERIGORD-CHALAIS.
LES MARQUISES
DE THUISKY,
DE SOMMERI,
DE MONTAGU.
LE DUC
DE GRAMMONT PAIR DE FRANCE
ET CAPTAINE DES GARDES DU CORPS DU ROI.
LES MARQUIS
DE LALLY-TOLENDAL PAIR DE FRANCE
ET MINISTRE D'ETAT.
DE LA TOUR DU PIN PAIR DE FRANCE
ET AMBASSADEUR A TURIN
DE CHABANNES PAIR DE FRANCE.
DE THUISY MARECHAL DES CAMPS ET ARMEES DU ROI
LE COMMANDER DE THUISY.

Applied on one side of the stem with British Royal Arms and on the other side with the arms of Dundas; the medallions on front and reverse inscribed *Hospitalité* and *Reconnaissance* respectively.

PROVENANCE
Sir David Dundas (1735-1820)
Sold Anonymously, Christie's New York, 23 October 1984, lot 372

Unfortunately it has not been possible to identify the specific occasion on which this cup was presented to Sir David Dundas, but it seems likely to have been a gift from the French nobility in recognition of his protection of their lives and property during the Napoleonic Wars. The presentation itself must date from 1819, the year the hallmarks on this cup were introduced or the following year, the year of Sir David's death.

Dundas's career in the army was distinguished by his writing the *Rules and Regulations for the Cavalry*, under which the armies of Abercromby, Moore and Wellington were disciplined. He succeeded his friend the Duke of York as Commander-in-Chief of the army in 1809 after the well-known scandal involving the selling of army commissions by the Duke of York's mistress, Mary Ann Clarke. In 1811, Dundas graciously stepped down in favour of the Duke who resumed his office.

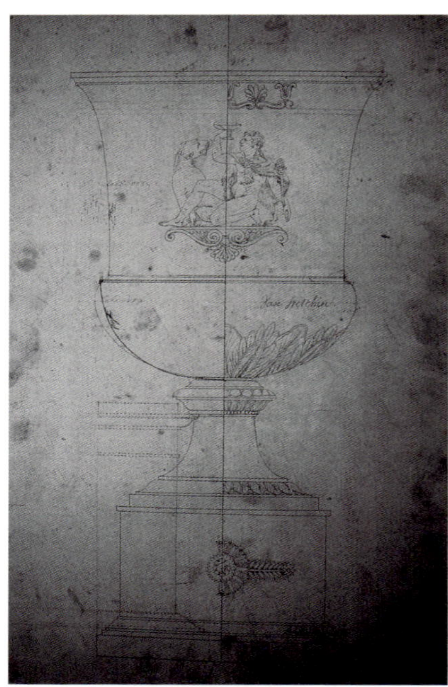

fig. 66 Design for a vase, by Prud'hon and Cavelier for Odiot, 1810-1811. *Courtesy Olivier Gaube du Gers, Odiot.*

fig. 67 Design for a vase by Henri Auguste for Odiot, circa 1806. *Courtesy Olivier Gaube du Gers, Odiot.*

The design for this cup is an interesting adaptation of one by Henri Auguste, circa 1806 (fig. 67). [1] The Auguste design was used for a pair of wine coolers set with enamel miniatures of the Shah of Persia and of the Imperial arms, presumably intended as a diplomatic gift from Napoleon, but the pair became part of the collection of Prince Louis Napoleon, later Napoleon III. [2]

Auguste, Biennais and Odiot were the leading silversmiths of the post-Revolutionary period. Auguste is perhaps the most interesting of the three, bridging the gap of the *ancien régime* and the Empire as well as influencing English Regency designs (see introduction, p. 8). He was born in 1759, and in 1785 obtained the succession to the official appointment as *orfèvre du Roi*, the post previously held by his father, the important goldsmith, Robert-Joseph Auguste. Henri Auguste was one of the most successful silversmiths immediately preceding the Revolution, lightening the heavy neo-classical style of his father by introducing arguably more elegant forms. He worked on commissions for Napoleon but by 1806 had incurred debts of some 1,370,000 francs. Although his creditors allowed him eight years to put his affairs in order, he nonetheless was caught at Dieppe trying to ship his stock and valuables to England under an assumed name. Finally, he was declared fraudulently bankrupt and sentenced to six years in irons. He died at Port-au-Prince in 1816.

Following Auguste's bankruptcy, his models and designs were put up for sale and Odiot acquired a great many of them. It would seem then that Odiot's designers reworked Auguste's drawing for the coolers which were to be given by Napoleon to the Shah. It is ironic that the same design was used both for a commission by Napoleon and for a presentation to a former enemy, the Commander-in-Chief of the British Army.

1. Illustrated by J-M Pinçon and O. Gaube du Gers, *Odiot l'orfèvre,* Paris, 1990, p.71, fig.95 and *Les grands orfèvres de Louis XIII à Charles X,* Paris, 1965, p.261.
2. *Ibid*, pls.1 and 2.

fig. 68 The arms of de la Chapelle as borne by Count Alfred de la Chapelle, who acquired pieces from the Demidoff Service around 1863, from a teapot by Odiot (cat.no.41)

THE DEMIDOFF SERVICE

The Demidoff service, one of the most magnificent French services of the early 19th century, is also one of the best documented. The account books of the firm of Odiot record that the service was ordered by "M. de Demidoff," identified as Count Nikolai Demidoff, who was charged for the most important part of the service on October 5, 1817. It has been said of the Demidoff service that the individual objects "are not so much dishes and cruet frames as they are fully realized small sculptures. The technical brilliance of these figures was due . . . to the extraordinarily coordinated system that integrated the skills of the *fondeurs-ciselleurs* with those of the silversmiths." [1] The records of Maison Odiot indicate that a considerable number of artists were employed on the service, including designers Cavelier, Prud'hon, Moreau and Garneray, and modellers Chaudet, Dumont and Roquier. [2]

Some elements of the design of the Demidoff service, particularly of the major tureens, can be seen as a celebration of the defeat of Napoleon—a victory in which Demidoff had played his part. [3] For example, the kneeling Nike figures beneath the tureens in the service (cat. no. 43) and the figures of Fame, Bacchus and Ceres supporting the bowl of the *pot-à-oille* (cat. no.42) can be seen in this light. It is somewhat ironic that the most "Napoleonic" of services should include elements celebrating his defeat, and that just two years afterwards it was exhibited at the Louvre. The catalogue for this exhibition, l'*Exposition des produits de l'industrie française au Louvre*, stated that "It has been a pleasure to see a fine silver-gilt service ordered by M. Demidoff, for which the estimated price is not less than 130,000 francs. Sixty pieces were counted, all decorated with bas-reliefs in exquisite taste, of subjects representing festivities. The main vases are supported by perfectly designed and worked figures, representing Bacchus, Ceres, Pomone etc. It is doubtful whether the art of the silversmith has ever produced anything more magnificent." [4]

Demidoff, born near St. Petersburg in 1773, entered

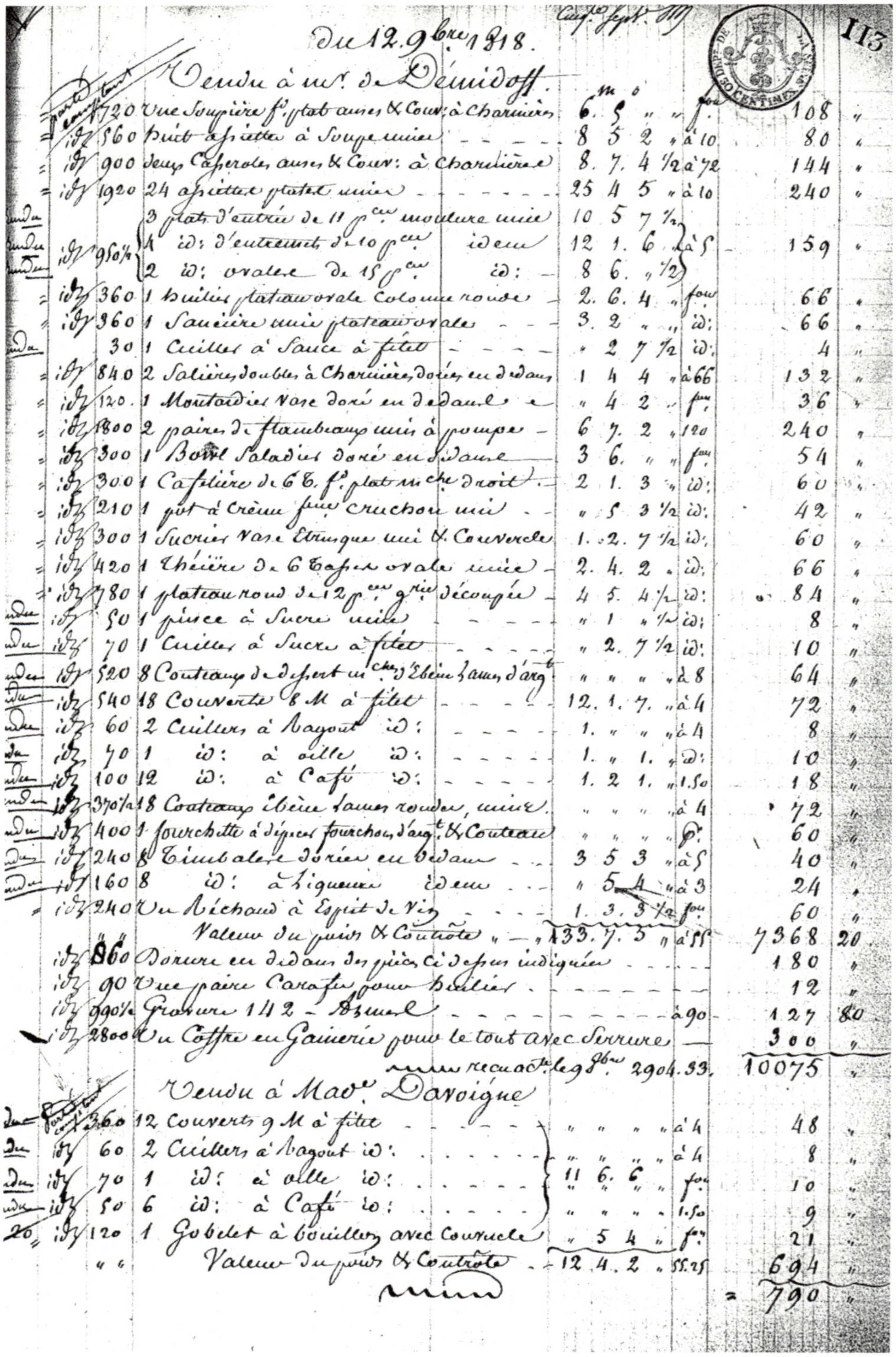

fig. 69 Odiot's account for "Mon. du Demidoff" dated 1818, one of at least three separate bills to Count Nikolai Demidoff by the firm between 1817 and 1820. *Courtesy Olivier Gaube du Gers, Odiot.*

the Imperial Guard at a young age and was aide-de-camp to Prince Potemkin in 1789. Within three years he had risen to the rank of Lieutenant-Colonel in the Grenadier Regiment of Moscow, and in 1794 he was made a Gentleman of the Bedchamber. He married into the powerful Stroganoff family. When retired from the army, he developed mines and ironworks on his own lands with great success. On the invasion of Russia by Napoleon, Demidoff raised his own regiment and returned to the army fighting at the battle of Borodino. His collection of paintings and natural curiosities survived the burning of Moscow, and these he donated to Moscow University. In 1815 he moved to Paris where his house soon became a center for leading academic and literary figures of his day. He was also known for his philanthropy, distributing 2000 francs a month to the poor of the city. For health reasons, he settled in Italy, where he began building the Villa of San Donato. Following his death in 1828 this work was completed by his son Anatole, Prince of San Donato, who married Jerome Napoleon's daughter. In 1859 Anatole moved to Paris, and from 1863 parts of the San Donato collection were sold both privately and by public auction. One of the first items to be sold privately was the magnificent silver-gilt dinner service ordered by his father.

There remain in the Odiot archives a number of accounts from 1817 through 1820 describing Nikolai Demidoff's purchases (fig. 69). From these there can be no doubt that he was indeed the original owner of the service, although all the pieces are either applied or engraved with later coats-of-arms. The applied arms are struck on the reverse with the maker's mark of English silversmith C. F. Hancock and London hallmarks of 1863. [5] There remains in the Hancock archives a photograph of the service with the later arms entitled "A Silver-gilt Dessert Service Made for and Purchased from Prince Demidoff," confirming that Hancock's actually owned the service when they applied the later arms. [6]

Although the 1863 coats-of-arms have never been previously identified, the noted French heraldry expert Philippe Palasi has now unravelled this mystery. [7] When the service was sold in 1928 at the Anderson Galleries in New York, it was described as the property of "an anonymous English Gentleman of Title." The introduction to the catalogue states that the service was acquired from the descendants of Madame de la Chapelle, to whom it had been given by Demidoff. This provenance, however, is only partly correct. Palasi has shown that the arms, though improperly emblazoned, are indeed those of de la Chapelle, as borne by the Counts of Morton and Beaulieu in Périgord. He has identified the arms on the Demidoff Service as those of Alfred de la Chapelle (1830-1914), a colourful explorer, adventurer, soldier, journalist, and politician. As a young man, de la Chapelle joined the California gold rush, but made his mining fortune at Coscopera, Mexico in the 1850s. In 1859 he returned to France and met the Empress of Russia among others, moving very much in the same society as both Anatole Demidoff and C.F. Hancock.

Obviously a restless individual, by 1860 de la Chapelle had emigrated to Australia where by 1867 he was back in the mining industry. In 1863 he is recorded as acknowledging an illegitimate son, Octave Xavier Alfred, whose mother Kate Royal was a twenty-year-old from Manchester. In 1889 the birth of a second child, Antoinette-Aline-Andrea de Morton de la Chapelle, was recorded at the French consulate in Dublin. Alfred de la Chapelle died in Essex in 1914, when it appears that the silver-gilt service was acquired by an Englishman, presumably the "Gentleman of Title" cited in the New York auction catalogue in 1928.

1. Clare Le Corbeiller, "An Introduction to Napoleonic Silver," in the exhibition catalogue, *The Arts Under Napoleon*, The Metropolitan Museum of Art, New York, 1978.
2. J-M Pinçon and O. Gaube du Gers, *Odiot l'orfèvre*, Paris, 1990.
3. This interpretation first appears in the exhibition catalogue, *The Glory of the Goldsmith*, Christie's, London, 1989, p. 36.
4. *Ibid*., p.36, where the French text is translated.
5. Clare Le Corbeiller, "The Construction of some Empire Silver," *The Metropolitan Museum Journal*, 1982 no. 16, p.198.
6. For a discussion of Hancock's ownership of the service, see Sotheby's, Geneva, 16 May 1994, lot 136.
7. We are extremely grateful to Philippe Palasi for allowing us to publish for the first time the results of his research. Mr. Palasi will publish a much more extensive article on the subject in a forthcoming issue of *Arts Decoratifs*.

41. A FRENCH TEAPOT WITH MOTHER-OF-PEARL HANDLE FROM THE DEMIDOFF SERVICE

Based on a drawing by Auguste Moreau
Maker's mark of Jean-Baptiste-Claude Odiot
Paris, 1798-1809

Height 7 in. (18 cm.)
Gross weight 42 oz. (1,316 gr.)

Engraved circa 1863 with a variation of the arms of de la Chapelle *accolé* with an alternate version of de la Chapelle, as borne by Count Alfred de la Chapelle

PROVENANCE
Count Nikolai Demidoff (1773-1828)
Anatole Demidoff, Prince of San Donato (1812-1870), until circa 1863
Charles Frederick Hancock, London, 1863
Count Alfred de la Chapelle, Seigneur of Morton and Beaulieu, Périgord (1830-1914)
An English Gentleman of Title, the Anderson Galleries, New York, 15 December 15 1928, lot 36

From the various accounts in his name and the number of surviving pieces, it appears that Demidoff ordered several tea services from Odiot. This teapot follows fairly closely a design in the Odiot archives except for the finial (fig. 70). A three-piece tea and coffee service, also with the de la Chapelle arms, is recorded, and includes a spherical teapot with serpent handle and small bud finial. [1] Sometime between 1819 and 1838, Odiot repeated the design of the latter teapot with a variation to the handle in another tea service with "Etruscan" style sugar basin and hot water jug. [2] This continuation of earlier designs and motifs is typical of Odiot's work.

1. Christie's, Geneva, 13 November 1995, lot 192.
2. Christie's, Geneva, 15 May 1995, lot 134.

fig. 70 Design for a teapot, by Auguste Moreau for Odiot, 1816-1817. *Courtesy Olivier Gaube du Gers, Odiot.*

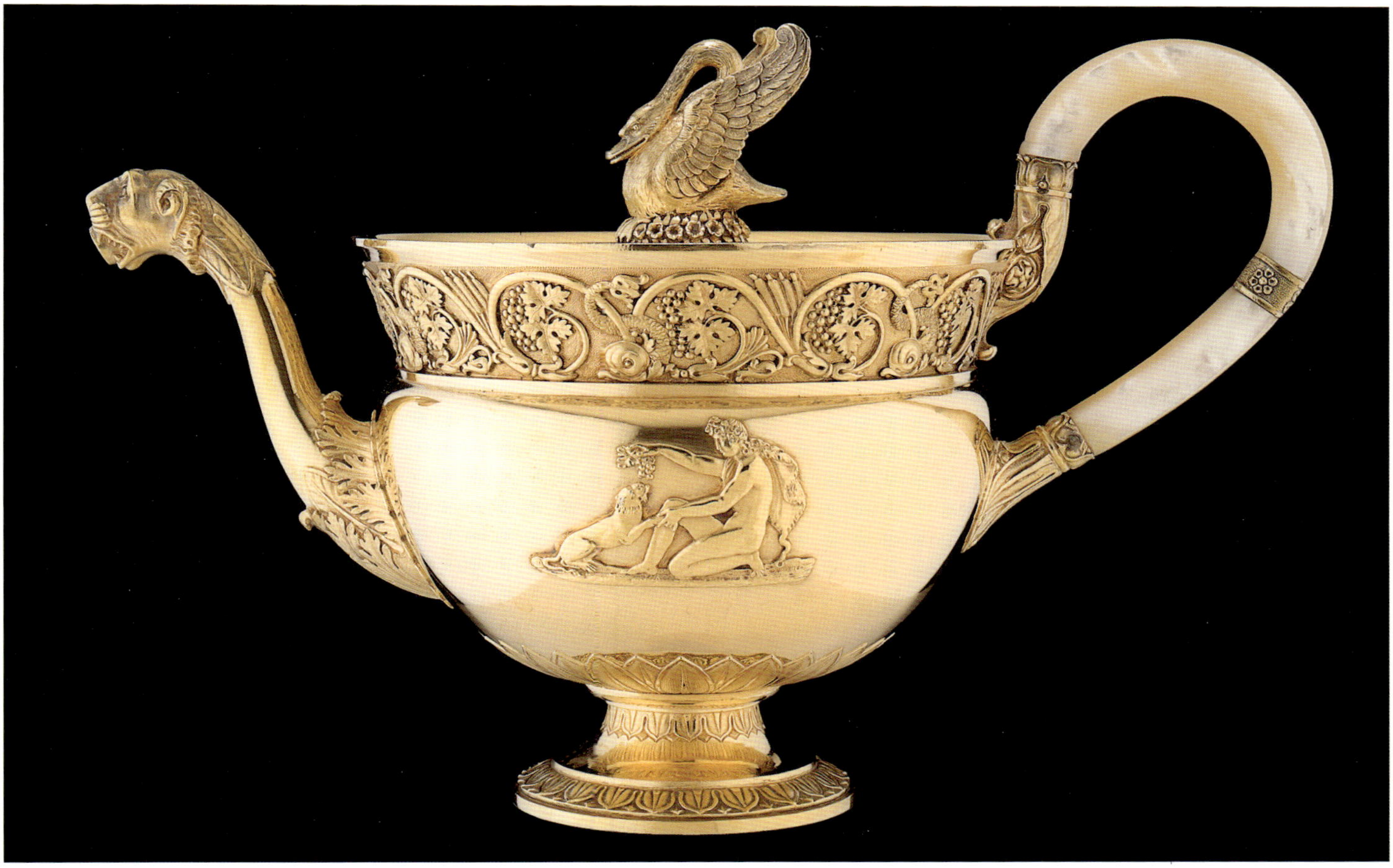

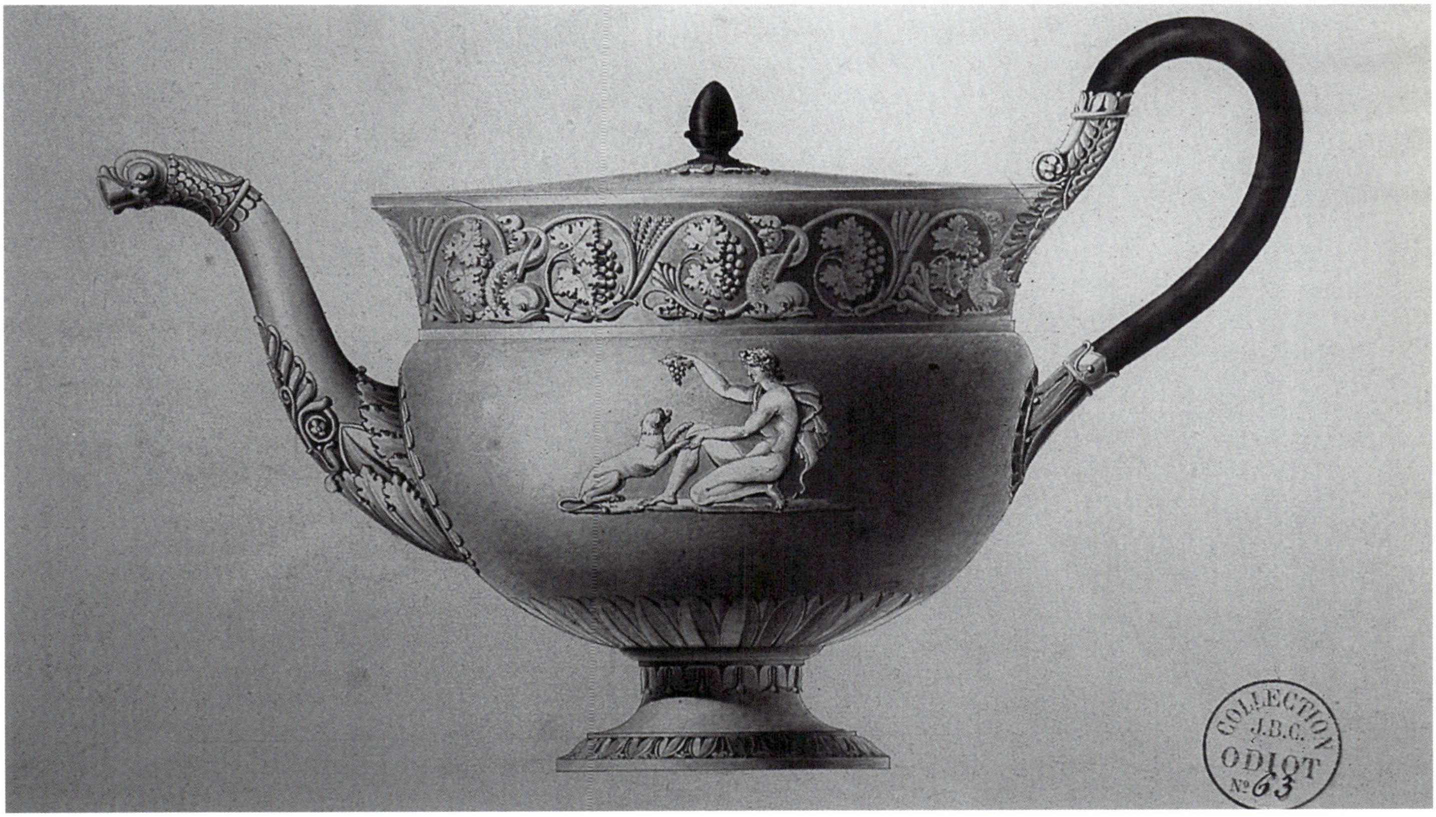
COLLECTION
J.B.C.
ODIOT
Nº 63

42. A FRENCH *POT-A-OILLE* FROM THE DEMIDOFF SERVICE

Based on a drawing by Adrien-Louis-Marie Cavelier
Maker's mark of Jean-Baptiste-Claude Odiot
Paris, 1817
The applied arms with maker's mark of Charles Frederick Hancock and hallmarks for London, 1863

Height 20 ½ in. (52 cm.)
Weight 547 oz. (17,016 gr.)

The arms are a variation of those of de la Chapelle *accolé* with an alternate version of de la Chapelle, as borne by Count Alfred de la Chapelle

PROVENANCE
Count Nikolai Demidoff (1773-1867)
Anatole Demidoff, Prince of San Donato (1812-1870), until probably circa 1863
Charles Frederick Hancock, London, 1863
Count Alfred de la Chapelle, Seigneur of Morton and Beaulieu, Périgord (1830-1914)
An English Gentleman of Title, the Anderson Galleries, New York, 15 December 1928, either lot 42 or 43

This magnificent *pot-à-oille* is identical to the example in the Al-Tajir Collection, and together they are the largest and most imposing pieces in the Demidoff service. [1] The pair is described in the original Odiot account of 1817 as "*2 Pots à oille, 3 femme debout c[omme] dessin 5000fr.*"

A drawing by Cavelier exists for a nearly identical tureen, although with handles formed as swans rather than snakes, around 1818. [2] Odiot used these swan handles on his other great dinner service of this period, that made for Count Branicki in 1819. [3]

Adrien-Louis-Marie Cavelier (1785-1867) was an architect and draftsman who made designs for both the silversmithing firm of Odiot and the bronze-foundry Thomire. It is known that both Odiot and Pierre-Philippe Thomire (1751-1843) collaborated on the dressing-table and mirror made for the Empress Marie-Louise in 1810 (subsequently destroyed on her order in 1832) and the cradle made for the King of Rome in 1811; in both cases they used drawings by Cavelier after designs by Prud'hon.[4] Thomire also made a magnificent malachite and gilt-bronze vase over 5 ½ feet high for Count Demidoff in 1819. [5] Clearly Odiot was familiar with the techniques of bronze makers—in particular those supplying furniture mounts—and, as Clare Le Corbeiller has pointed out, used them in the construction of his silver. [6]

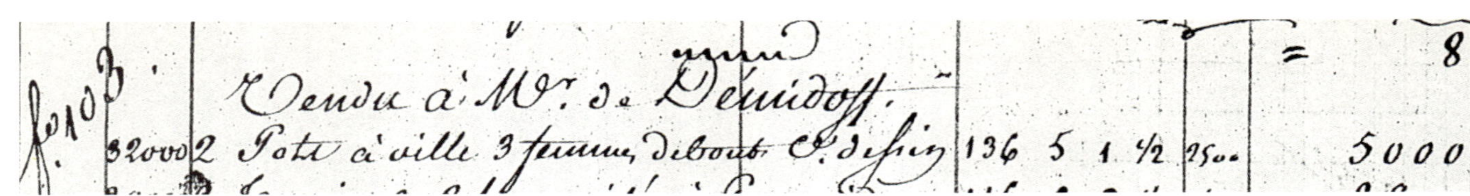
Vendu à Mr. de Demidoff.
32000 2 Pots à oille 3 figures, debout. P. d'esprit 136 5 1 ½ 250. 5000

fig. 71 Odiot's description of the pair of *pots-à-oille* in the accounts for the Demidoff Service, 1817. *Courtesy Olivier Gaube du Gers, Odiot.*

1. The *pot-à-oille* in the Al-Tajir Collection was formerly in the collection of Anna Thomson Dodge, Detroit and was sold Christie's, London, 23 June 1971, lot 50. It is also discussed in the Exhibition Catalogue, The *Glory of the Goldsmith,* London, 1989, p. 36 no 21a. *Pots-à-oille* date to the late 17th century, and were intended to hold stews or ragouts, newly fashionable in France at that time.
2. Jean-Marie Pinçon and Olivier Gaube du Gers, *Odiot L'Orfèvre,* Paris, 1990, p. 67, pls. 87 and 88.
3. See Christie's New York, 28 April 1992 lot 31, for an illustration published by Moleon in 1824 of pieces from the Branicki Service, including the swan-handled *pot-à-oille* exhibited at the Louvre by Odiot in 1819. The service was ordered by Countess Branicka, the niece of Prince Potemkin and wife of the Polish Count François-Xavier Petrovich Branicki. After her death in 1838, the history of the service is obscure. Some of it was given by Adam Branicki to the state in the 1920s and remains on view at Wilanow. A large part of the service was acquired by the German banker Dr. Fritz Mannheimer. He subsequently settled in Amsterdam and much of his part of the service is now in the Rijksmuseum. Among pieces from the Branicki service to appear at auction are a pair of tureens from the Love collection (fig. 27), sold at Christie's, New York, 28 April 1992, lot 31, now in a private European collection; a large oval tureen, Sotheby's, Geneva, 12 November 1990, lot 98; a sugar-bowl and cover, Christie's, Geneva, 12 May 1987, lot 107, now in the Al-Tajir Collection (illustrated in the exhibition catalogue, *The Glory of the Goldsmith,* London, 1989, p.42, no. 25); and a wine cooler, Sotheby's, New York, 5 November 1986, lot 72.
4. Pinçon and Gaube du Gers, *op. cit.,* pp.105-107.
5. Exhibition catalogue, *The Arts under Napoleon,* The Metropolitan Museum of Art, New York, 1978, no. 182 (acc. no. 44.152).
6. Clare Le Corbeiller, "The Construction of Some Empire Silver," *The Metropolitan Museum Journal,* 1982, no. 16, pp. 195-198.

fig. 72 Design for a *pot-à-oille*, by A-L-M Cavelier for Odiot, 1807. *Courtesy Olivier Gaube du Gers, Odiot.*

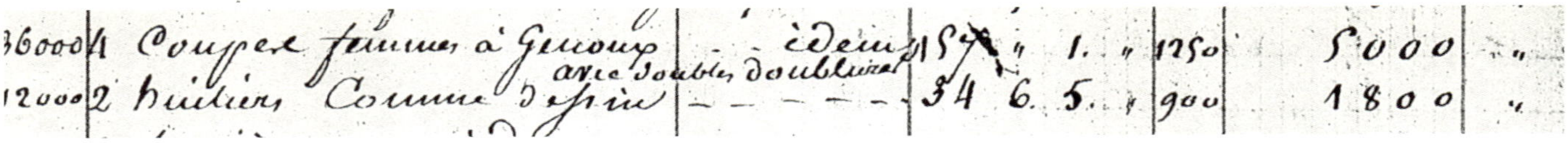

fig. 73 Odiot's description of the tureens in the accounts for the Demidoff Service, 1817. *Courtesy Olivier Gaube du Gers, Odiot.*

43. A PAIR OF FRENCH TUREENS OR *COUPES D'ENTREMETS* FROM THE DEMIDOFF SERVICE

Based on a drawing by Adrien-Louise-Marie Cavelier
Maker's mark of Jean-Baptiste-Claude Odiot
Paris, 1817
The applied arms with maker's mark of Charles Frederick Hancock and hallmarks for London, 1863

Height 15 ½ in. (39.5 cm.)
Weight 588 oz. (18,305 gr.)

The arms are a variation of those of de la Chapelle *accolé* with an alternate version of de la Chapelle, as borne by Count Alfred de la Chapelle

PROVENANCE
Count Nikolai Demidoff (1773-1828)
Anatole Demidoff, Prince of San Donato (1812-1870), probably until circa 1863
Charles Frederick Hancock, London, 1863
Count Alfred de la Chapelle, Seigneur of Morton and Beaulieu, Périgord (1830-1914)
An English Gentleman of Title, the Anderson Galleries, New York, December 15, 1928, either lot 46 (a pair) or 47 (a pair)
Possibly Mrs. Rockefeller McCormick, American Art Association/Anderson Galleries Inc., New York, January 6, 1934, lots 823 (a single) and 824 (a single)
Isabel Van Wie Willys, Parke-Bernet Galleries, New York, October 27, 1945, either lot 220 (a pair) or 221 (a pair)

EXHIBITED
The Metropolitan Museum of Art, New York, "The Arts Under Napoleon", April 6-July 30, 1978, cat. no.156, fig 32.

LITERATURE
Clare Le Corbeiller, "The Construction of Some Empire Silver," *The Metropolitan Museum Journal,* 1982, no. 16, pp. 195-198 and figs. 4-6.

These superb circular tureens are from a set of four (figs. 74 and 75). The other two, formerly in the Love Collection, are now in the Al-Tajir Collection. [1] Together with the two *pots-à-oilles* (one, cat. no. 42) and a larger pair of oval tureens of similar design, they are the quintessence of the Napoleonic style. [2] The four tureens appear in the original Odiot account of 1817 as

> *4 Coupes femmes à genoux idem [i.e., comme dessin] 5000fr. avec double doublement*

Although described in the Demidoff account as "*coupes*," their function may be inferred from the Odiot account of 1819 for the Branicki service where the almost identical pieces are called "*4 Casserole Coupes idem [i.e., femmes à genoux] avec dble dblement.*" However, Odiot's accounts describe similar tureens as vegetable dishes, *soupières*, and most frequently *coupes d'entremets*. Whatever their practical function, these tureens were above all intended for display, and in this they brilliantly succeed.

1. Sold from the Love Collection, Christie's, New York, 14 June, 1982, lot 143 and described in the exhibition catalogue, *The Glory of the Goldsmith,* London, 1989, p.36, cat. no.21c.
2. One oval tureen was sold anonymously, Christie's, Geneva, 9 November, 1976, lot 277, the other was from an American Private Collection, Sotheby's, New York, 28 October 1987, lot 164. Both are now in the Al-Tajir Collection, described and illustrated in the exhibition catalogue, *The Glory of the Goldsmith, op. cit.,* pp. 36-37, cat. no.21b.

fig. 74 Design for a tureen or a *coupe d'entremet* from the Demidoff Service, by A-L-M Cavelier for Odiot, circa 1816. *Courtesy Olivier Gaube du Gers, Odiot.*

fig. 75 Design for a tureen or *coupe d'entremet* from the Demidoff Service, by A-L-M Cavelier for Odiot, circa 1816, inscribed "*approuvé*" to indicate acceptance of the design by the client. *Courtesy Olivier Gaube du Gers, Odiot.*

44. A FRENCH LADLE FROM THE DEMIDOFF SERVICE

Maker's mark of François-Dominique Naudin
Paris, 1817

Length 14 in. (35.5 cm.)
Weight 8 oz. (271 gr.)

Engraved circa 1863 with a variation of the arms of de la Chapelle *accolé* with an alternate version of de la Chapelle, as borne by Count Alfred de la Chapelle

PROVENANCE
Count Nikolai Demidoff (1773-1828)
Anatole Demidoff, Prince of San Donato (1812-1870), probably until circa 1863
Charles Frederick Hancock, London, 1863
Count Alfred de la Chapelle, Seigneur of Morton and Beaulieu, Périgord (1830-1914)
An English Gentleman of Title, the Anderson Galleries, New York, 15 December, 1928, either lot 71 or 72

This fine ladle appears to be one of a pair listed in the 1817 Odiot account as "*2 id [i.e., cuillers] à l'oille id [? richée brunie] 24fr.*"

The manufacture of table silver was a specialized craft, and in both France and England such specialists supplied knives, forks and spoons to complete large dinner services by other makers. In this case, Odiot must have paid Naudin for the work and added a commission before retailing the service to Demidoff.

45. A PAIR OF FRENCH DOUBLE SALT CELLARS FROM THE DEMIDOFF SERVICE

Based on a drawing by Adrien-Louise-Marie Cavelier after a design by Charles Percier
Maker's mark of Jean-Baptiste-Claude Odiot
Paris, 1809-1819
The applied arms with maker's mark of Charles Frederick Hancock and hallmarks for London, 1863

Height 9 ¾ in. (25 cm.)
Weight 82 oz. (2,574 gr.)

The arms are a variation of those of de la Chapelle *accolé* with an alternate version of de la Chapelle, as borne by Count Alfred de la Chapelle

PROVENANCE
Count Nikolai Demidoff (1773-1828)
Anatole Demidoff, Prince of San Donato (1812-1870), until probably circa 1863
Charles Frederick Hancock, London, 1863
Count Alfred de la Chapelle, Seigneur of Morton and Beaulieu, Périgord (1830-1914)
An English Gentleman of Title, the Anderson Galleries, New York, 15 December 1928, either lot 51 or 52

fig. 76 Design for an-oil-and vinegar frame by Charles Percier, from Armand Guérinet, ed., *Recueil de dessins d'orfèvrerie du Premier Empire, par Biennais, orfèvre de Napoléon Ier et de la Couronne*, Paris, 1911, pl. 45. *Courtesy New York Public Library.*

fig. 77 Design for a salt cellar by A-L-M Cavelier after Charles Percier for Odiot, circa 1817, inscribed "*approuvé*" to indicate acceptance of the design by the client. *Courtesy Olivier Gaube du Gers, Odiot.*

fig. 78 Design for a salt cellar, by A-L-M Cavelier after Charles Percier for Odiot, circa 1817. *Courtesy Olivier Gaube du Gers, Odiot.*

A pair of gilt-bronze salt cellars in the Musée des Arts Décoratifs with similar handles formed as the standing figures of Venus Fortuna and Mars are, like the present salt cellars, based on a Percier design reworked by Cavelier (figs. 76-78). [1] Both Odiot and Biennais used this design, and a number of examples made for different clients by Odiot are known. The central standing figure holding billowing drapery is reminiscent of the superb figure of Leda and the Swan which forms the handles of two oil-and-vinegar frames from the Demidoff service drawn by Garneray, also to a Percier design. [2] The frames were included in the 1817 Demidoff invoice, at 1800fr, and were formerly in the Love Collection (fig. 25). [3]

1. The gilt-bronze examples are illustrated in Jean-Marie Pinçon and Olivier Gaube du Gers, *Odiot l'orfèvre,* Paris, 1990, fig. 120, p. 84.
2. *Ibid.*, p. 172.
3. These cruets were given by the Love Foundation to the Metropolitan Museum of Art, where they were exhibited in "The Arts Under Napoleon" 6 April-30 July 1978, cat. no. 159. Odiot gave a bronze version of these frames to the Musée du Luxembourg for instructional purposes in 1817. Clare Le Corbeiller discusses them in "The Construction of some Empire Silver," *The Metropolitan Museum Journal,* 1982, no. 16, pp. 195-198, figs.1-3.

INDEX

All numbers refer to page numbers; boldface indicates an illustration